HAUNTED PUBS AND HOTELS OF WORCESTERSHIRE AND ITS BORDERS INCLUDING HENLEY IN ARDEN AND STOURBRIDGE

ANNE BRADFORD

With best wishes

Anne Bradford

November 2000

Hunt End Books

Although, in many cases, the christian names only of contributors have been given,
if anyone would like to contact any one of them they can do so through the publisher.

Hunt End Books, 66 Enfield Road, Hunt End, Redditch, Worcestershire, B97 5NH, England. Telephone: 01527 542516. **First published** November 1998. **ISBN** 0 9519481 3 X. **Pub photography** by Anne, John, Edwin Bradford.
Still life photography by Edwin Bradford. **Design** by Edwin Bradford. **Printed** in Great Britain by Redwood Books Limited, Kennet Way, Trowbridge, Wiltshire BA14 8RN. This book is sold subject to the condition that it shall not, by way of

Other books by the same author: Midland Ghosts and Hauntings, by Anne Bradford and Barrie Roberts, published by Quercus, 1994;
Haunted Worcestershire, published by Hunt End Books, 1996; **Royal Enfield,** published by Amulree, 1996; **Midland Spooks and Spectres,** by Anne Bradford and Barrie Roberts, published by Quercus, 1998;
An Old History of Redditch by William Avery, with illustrations by Norman Neasom.

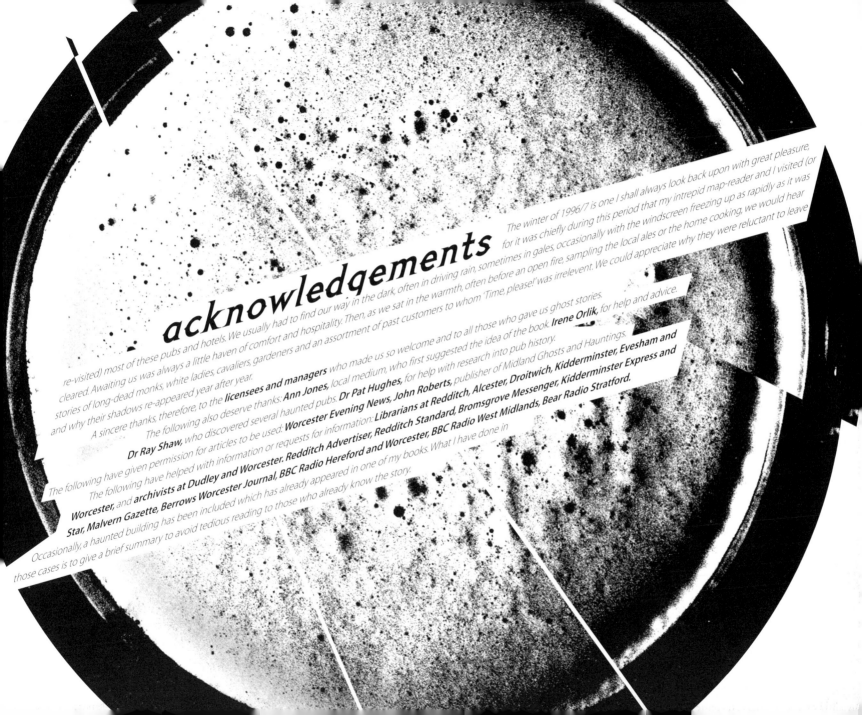

acknowledgements

The winter of 1996/7 is one I shall always look back upon with great pleasure, for it was chiefly during this period that my intrepid map-reader and I visited (or re-visited) most of these pubs and hotels. We usually had to find our way in the dark, often in driving rain, sometimes in gales, occasionally with the windscreen freezing up as rapidly as it was cleared. Awaiting us was always a little haven of comfort and hospitality. Then, as we sat in the warmth, often before an open fire, sampling the local ales or the home cooking, we would hear stories of long-dead monks, white ladies, cavaliers, gardeners and an assortment of past customers to whom 'Time, please!' was irrelevent. We could appreciate why they were reluctant to leave and why their shadows re-appeared year after year.

A sincere thanks, therefore, to the **licensees and managers** who made us so welcome and to all those who gave us ghost stories. **Irene Orlik,** for help and advice.

The following also deserve thanks: *Ann Jones,* local medium, who first suggested the idea of the book. **Dr Pat Hughes,** for help with research into pub history. **Dr Ray Shaw,** who discovered several haunted pubs. **Worcester Evening News, John Roberts,** publisher of Midland Ghosts and Hauntings.

The following have given permission for articles to be used: **Worcester Evening News, John Roberts,** publisher for information: **Librarians at Redditch, Alcester, Droitwich, Kidderminster, Evesham and Worcester,** and **archivists at Dudley and Worcester. Redditch Advertiser, Redditch Standard, Bromsgrove Messenger, Kidderminster Express and Star, Malvern Gazette, Berrows Worcester Journal,** BBC Radio Hereford and Worcester, BBC Radio West Midlands, Bear Radio Stratford.

Occasionally, a haunted building has been included which has already appeared in one of my books. What I have done in those cases is to give a brief summary to avoid tedious reading to those who already know the story.

Dudley

Warley

Kinver Stourbridge

Clent

Caunsall

Romsley

Kidderminster

Bewdley

Stourport on Severn

Bromsgrove

Newnham Bridge

Webheath

Reddiitch

Abberley

Henley in Arden

Hanbury

Droitwich

Studley

Feckenham

Astwood Bank

Clifton on Teme

Claines

Tibberton

Inkberrow

Alcester

Stratford
upon Avon

Worcester

Salford Priors

Pershore

Bretforton

Hanley Castle

Evesham

Upton upon Severn

Worcestershire

contents
Pub Guide; History;

‡These stories are also covered in HAUNTED WORCESTERSHIRE, Hunt End Books, 1996

beers

telephone

other information

food

garden

Opening times

directions

children

pub guide

These stories have been compiled between 1992 and 1998, although most places were revisited during the winter of 1997/78. In March 1998 a questionaire was sent to every pub or hotel involved and the information received is given as a brief pub guide at the beginning of each story.

Directions have only been included when the pub or hotel is not easy to find or not in the centre of the appropriate village. Every effort has been made to check factual statements but if every piece of information were to be checked the book would never have been completed. We have

therefore had to rely at times on information from the landlord or the regulars.

history

So many public houses have referred to the battle of Worcester, it will probably be helpful if we give a brief summary of developments. The Civil War revolved around Charles I and the Battle of Worcester around his son, Charles II. Worcestershire was involved in the civil war of the 1600's more than any other county, and Worcester more than any other town. It lay at the meeting point of six vital roads and on a place of crossing over the Severn. It was also en route between the King's headquarters at Oxford, and Wales, which sent money and provisions to the King. In the last year of the civil war Worcester was under siege for two months. By a strange quirk of fate, the first skirmish in 1642 and most of the last battle of the war, the Battle of Worcester, took place at Powick Bridge, just outside Worcester.

The Civil War (1642 to 1646)
Disagreements between Charles I and his people, the Parliamentarians, flared into civil war in 1642. The first great battle was at Edgehill in the Cotswolds, where each side claimed victory. Four years later, in 1649, Charles I was charged with treason and executed. By 1646, the Royalists had been thoroughly defeated. Then Oliver Cromwell created his New Model Army and by 1646, the Royalists had been thoroughly defeated.

The Battle of Worcester
The historian, J W Willis Bund, describes the Battle of Worcester as 'the last, the greatest and the fiercest battle of them all'.

While imprisoned, Charles I schemed with Scotland to restore him to the throne, but the plots were discovered and he was eventually executed. The Scots decided to annoy Cromwell by provisionally proclaiming Charles I's son (also named Charles) as king, despite the fact that he was in exile in Europe. Two years later Charles returned to Scotland where he was officially crowned as King of Scotland. An army of 15,000 Scots was raised and Charles left Stirling on July 1651 to invade England. He marched through Lancashire, appealing for support on the way, and entered Worcester on August 22nd. The battle took place on 3rd September 1651. Cromwell had 28,000 men to the king's 16,000. By the end of the day there was nothing left of the Scottish army; 3,000 were dead at the Wick or Sidbury gate, 10,000 were prisoners and the remainder had run for their lives. The number of wounded was so great that they were never counted. Charles was extremely lucky to escape alive and spent a hair-raising six weeks on the run before he managed to reach France.

In 1658 Oliver Cromwell died and the Republic began to fall apart. Charles was asked to return to England to be crowned. He entered London in 1660 on his 30th birthday to become Charles II.

Details of the Battle of Worcester can be seen at the Commandery (which is almost opposite the Cathedral) in Worcester.

Manor Arms

NESTLING AMONG THE GENTLE ABBERLEY HILLS IS THE TINY VILLAGE OF ABBERLEY.
At the heart of the village is an ancient Church, still in use. The tower walls on the western side and the south doorway, together with other bits and pieces, date back to the 1100's. It was here, in the early 1960's, that twelfth century spoons were found which are now in the British Museum. Opposite the Church is the ancient Manor Arms Hotel, known to be at least 300 years old and so near to the Church that a brewhouse must surely have existed for centuries on this site to provide the Church with ale.

The *Worcestershire Village Book* reports that the 'ghost of the 'Grey Lady' inhabits the Church and the nearby Rectory. The locals say that the area is haunted by the apparition of a girl who gave birth to an illegitimate child at a time when it was such a disgrace that she murdered the baby and committed suicide.

In May 1989, Andy Lacock, a twenty-three year old actor, was invited to dinner at the Manor Arms by the owners, John and Lita Kitley, and their daughter, Julie. After the meal, Andy decided to go for a stroll and had just reached the gate of the churchyard when:

I saw something **floating** towards  Abberley Church

I could not believe what I was seeing. I closed my eyes
and opened them again but it was still there. It was about
five or six feet off the floor, human size with a blue glow.
I dashed inside and told the others to come
and have a look. Then we stood and watched it
for a few seconds until it disappeared.

☎ **01299 896507**

Mon–Fri: 1200–1500
          1800–2300
Sat: 1100–2300
Sun: 1100–2230

Yes

Same menu throughout

Yes, also patio

Belongs to Enterprise Inns chain with nine rooms for letting. Special evening every other month eg Theme Food night, bands or quiz. Restaurant has French windows opening onto patio and magnificent views over Abberley Hills. In *Pub Walks in Worcestershire*.

ABBERLEY

Lord Nelson

ACCORDING TO LOCAL LEGENDS, ALCESTER HAS BEEN CURSED TWICE, IT IS SAID THAT THIS WHY IT HAS NEVER PROSPERED ENOUGH TO BECOME A LARGE TOWN (ALTHOUGH MANY PEOPLE MIGHT CONSIDER THIS TO BE A BLESSING). IT WAS SUPPOSEDLY CURSED BY SAINT CHAD, BECAUSE OF THE HOSTILE RECEPTION HE RECEIVED WHEN HE VISITED IN ABOUT THE YEAR 700, AND BY THE MONK ANSELM, WHO WAS MURDERED THERE IN THE 1100S. KING STEPHEN HAD BUILT A LARGE PRIORY THERE BUT QUARRELLED WITH THE MONKS AND ARRANGED TO HAVE ANSELM LIQUIDATED. PERHAPS THE CURSES HAD A SUPERNATURAL EFFECT ON THE TOWN BECAUSE MANY OF THE RESIDENTS HAVE A GHOST STORY OR TWO TO TELL, INCLUDING THE LICENSEES OF THE LORD NELSON.

Horatio Nelson triumphed at the battle of Trafalgar in 1805 when the Lord Nelson probably acquired its name, but it was built long before then and was originally a school. Florence Criddle lived there in the days before oak beams and low ceilings became desirable assets.

My husband's family managed the Lord Nelson at Alcester, we moved there in the late 1920's when I was about twenty. I hated the house. There was always a cold, dark atmosphere and things used to rumble about. My room was the one at the top and I always felt there was something in the bedroom with me. I couldn't sleep at nights and I'm not the imaginative kind. After I had left home my brother-in-law, Les Haydon, was put in that room whenever he stayed over night; he said something was there and in the end he refused to sleep in it.

I married my husband on 30th December 1935 and we had to stay at the Nelson temporarily because the place we were going to wasn't ready for us. My husband was always interested in anything paranormal and I think he was a bit psychic himself as he always knew if anyone had died. Four days after we were married he suddenly sat up in bed and said, 'Grannies just gone'. I asked,

'What do you mean?'. My grand-mother was very ill at the time and she had just passed away. Twelve months later my father-in-law also died and as he had kept the Nelson my husband took it over.

Something very strange happened the night that my father-in-law died. I was with him when he breathed his last. The woman who was laying him out said, 'Now you go downstairs while I do what I have to do, then I'll call you up again'. There were four of us downstairs, all relatives. We were sitting in the living room which was the smallest room in the house. A door led off from the living room into the bar where there was a row of bells so that a customer could summon the bartender and give him his order. Suddenly, one of the bells in the bar started ringing, a very violent ring, someone was really pulling it. We all looked flabber-gasted. Then I said, 'We're being stupid, it's a cat got in or

something' so we all went into the bar. We saw that it was the Smoke Room bell that had been rung, the bell was still swinging as if someone had given it a really good bang. We went into the Smoke Room but nobody was there. All the outside locks were fastened and no-one could have got in. We were very shaken and we agreed that dad was letting us know that he'd gone.

Only a few weeks later, in the February, my husband had double pneumonia and pleurisy and he was very, very poorly. I was expecting our first baby at the time and I was sitting in the bedroom with him when he opened his arms and said, 'I'm coming dad!'. He said later that he had seen his dad's head and shoulders come through the ceiling and he thought that his dad called him, it was very real. My mother-in-law was downstairs so I ran down and told her, she was a stout woman but she came running up the stairs two at a time. She took one look at him then she rushed downstairs into the yard where we let the old stables as garages. A man was there washing his car and she asked him to get the

doctor quickly. The older doctor was out but a young doctor came. He sent us downstairs but came down half-an-hour later and said he had managed to get him back.

My husband recovered and ran the Nelson until 1940.

The present landlord, Mark Brampton, says he's not surprised by Florence's story.

We have always suspected that there is something here. We have had strange things happen, especially in the cellar. The staff won't go down into the cellar on their own.

Our bottles of soft drinks—the orange juice etcetera—are kept in crates down the cellar. One morning we got up and the bottles had all been taken out of the crates and placed in rows. No-one could have gone down there overnight. That was dead weird.

Things (such as keys) go missing and then turn up somewhere so obvious that they couldn't have been there while you were looking for them. A few weeks ago somebody threw a dart, it fell out of the dart board and we're still looking for it.

ARROW MILL

Arrow Mill

THERE WAS A MILL ON THIS SITE AS FAR BACK AS 1086, BUT THE PRESENT BUILDING DATES FROM AROUND 1800.

The mill has a long history of ghosts. The first one goes back to 1477, in the time of the Wars of the Roses, when the nobility were at each others' throats. The mill was owned by Thomas Burdett who had a tame white buck of which he was very fond. Unfortunately, when Edward IV went hunting, he shot this pet deer. Thomas said a few choice words about the king which his enemies lost no time in relaying to the king's ears, with the result that Thomas had his head chopped off. Consequently, the first ghost is a white buck followed by a bodiless head.

This ghost changed the whole history of Britain. Thomas was very friendly with the king's brother, the Duke of Clarence, who made so much fuss about the execution that the king and his youngest brother, Richard, decided to do away with the Duke. They were very gentlemanly about it and asked him how he would like to be killed. He chose to be drowned in a vat of Malmsey wine, consequently the incident is known as the Malmsey Butt. This meant that when the king died, only his two small sons barred the path of Richard III from the throne. These were the poor little princes in the Tower who mysteriously disappeared.

When Simon Woodhams took over the present mill he was warned about the grey lady which his predecessor found to be quite a nuisance. The story goes that at one time, perhaps during the sixteenth or seventeenth century, two sisters ran the mill. One of them was caught up in the machinery and killed, hence the grey lady.

In the middle of the last century, the miller upstream at Oversley had an argument with his wife which came to a grisly end when he chopped her head off and threw it into the river Alne. It floated downstream and wedged in the sluice at Arrow Mill.

It is said that, from time to time, the **RIVER** occasionally **RUNS RED**

The final ghost story occurred in the October of 1991. The bar manager had had a very busy weekend. The rest of the staff had gone home and he was in the Gun Bar just putting the final odds and ends away in the early hours of the Sunday morning when something caught his eye. He turned round but nothing was there. Something again caught his eye and this time, when he turned round, he saw the shadow of a man standing there. He described it as follows :

It was just standing there, with the arms a little way out from the sides. It was a dark shape of a man, quite solid, I couldn't see through it. He was about five feet eight inches in height and quite a heavy man. I couldn't see any details, only dark shapes where the eyes would have been. I didn't wait to see if it faded, I threw the keys into the safe and ran for the car.

The bar manager refused to go back into the Gun Bar and he found a post at another hotel.

☎ **01789 762419**

 The Arrow Mill was once part of the Ragley estate and is just across the road from the entrance to Ragley Hall.

Yes

 Restaurant and bar meals

Sixty acres of garden including mill pound, weir and river

 Local guest beers

ⓘ Eighteen en suite rooms. Workings of old mill converted into water feature in restaurant. Events almost every weekend, such as weddings, car club events, etc. Featured in Johannes Hanson's *Best Loved Hotels of the World* ('Believe it or not', says Simon Woodhams, the owner).

ALCESTER

Bell *and the* Woodman

AT THE SIDE OF THE BELL PUBLIC HOUSE IS A LAWN AND ON THIS LAWN THERE ONCE stood another pub, The Woodman. This was demolished round about 1964. It was a very old coaching inn dating back to the 1700s. The funerals were always held in the Club Room and the locals will tell you that they had some very splendid wakes in there. An ex-regular of the Woodman, Colin Robinson, says:

The Woodman ghost was so well known that there was a plaque on the wall telling you about it. It was supposed to be a policeman, Brian Onens, who was once licensee there. He died when he fell from top to bottom of an outside staircase.

He had a WOODEN LEG and therefore WALKED WITH A LIMP

Strange things happened in the pub—they used to lock and bolt the doors at night and in the morning they would be open—but the ghost usually manifested itself by the sound of footsteps which were unmistakable because of the limp. You could hear them going across the ceiling and coming down the stairs. It would start one side and go across to the other but when you got to the top to have a look they would stop. When you were downstairs you could hear them upstairs and when you were upstairs you could hear them downstairs. If they were coming down the stairs and you went to the stairs, they stopped. We thought at one time it was something echoing from house to house but the people next door went on holiday for three weeks and the sounds continued. Sometimes you caught sight of a shadow and one or two people had seen him.

Rumour has it that at one time they thought of building a couple of houses on the land where the Woodman once stood but it was thought that the ghost would return to haunt them so the idea was dropped.

The locals say that when the Woodman was demolished, the ghost moved to the modern pub next door—the Bell. The move seems to have given it a new image, described here by John Heath.

I was working at the Bell in December 1996, helping to put things ready for Christmas. At about 10 o'clock in the morning, the chap who runs the place said to me, 'I've just got to pop out for a minute, help yourself to a drink while I'm away'. I poured myself a beer and walked towards the lounge. The next thing I knew there was this woman standing in the lounge. She was very attractive, I would say in her mid-thirties, slim, with long, straight, shoulder-length blonde hair and quite tall, probably about five feet eight. She was wearing a cream trouser suit which looked as if it belonged to the 1970's, with flared trousers and a flared jacket.

I asked if I could help her. She said, 'I just want a drink'. I told her that we weren't really open. She replied, 'I'll have some of yours then, please'. She sat down and I poured her some of my drink. I sat talking to her, I can't remember everything I said but I know that I asked her where she was from and what she was doing—the general kind of questions you ask when you meet someone in a pub. She said her name was Marion or Marianne or something like that. She felt like a friend, like someone I had known a long time ago. She was just

☎ 01527 892488

Mon–Sun:
Bar: 1200–1500
       1900–2300
Food: 1200–1400
       1900–2100

🍴 Mainly restaurant meals

Ⱥ Yes

giving vague answers. Then the landlord came back and said, 'Who the hell are you talking to?'. I answered, 'The lady there' and he said, 'There's nobody there, you're talking to thin air'. I said again, 'There she is, she's there' but when I looked across to where she had been sitting she had vanished. We searched the building but didn't find anybody and she couldn't have got out because the landlord had locked the door behind him as he came in. He told me that I was going round the twist. It was so weird. I would emphasise that I was stone cold sober and had only had a few sips when I first saw her.

I was quite gobsmacked. At first I thought, 'Am I cracking up?'. Then Layla said she had seen her as well.

Ever since then I have taken an interest in the paranormal. I read anything I can get my hands on and I watch all the paranormal programmes on the television in the hope that one day I will find an explanation to what I saw. Was it an hallucination or what?

Layla lived at the Bell for twelve months in about 1993 when her mother ran the Bell. She says:

When I lived here we had one or two strange things happening. We would switch the lights off at night and when we came down in the morning, the lights would be on again. Knives and forks and glasses would move. You would know without any doubt that you had put a glass in a certain place or laid the knife and fork on a certain table but it would all have been moved.

I was idly playing with the doors from the bar to the kitchen, pushing them open and swinging behind them, when I happened to look over to the other side of the room where the bar is divided from the lounge by a fairly open wooden screen. There stood a lady in an all-in-one, creamy white gown of some kind; I couldn't see her dress clearly but I could see her hair and features very clearly. She was quite thin and about thirtyish. Her blond hair was tied back and I saw her features so well I would know her again if I saw her. On went my personal panic button and I froze.

I thought, 'OH MY GOD', what's that?'

Then I looked again and she was gone

She was only there for a second or two. It was just the shock of it at first. I didn't say anything to anybody, I thought it must just be my wild imagination and then I heard of two other people who had seen her, Pete and John. It made Peter really ill when he saw her, I hear that he went as white as a sheet and ran out the back. Then my mother's friend, John, saw her in the passageway. He was very uptight about it, and not at all pleased about having seen a ghost. I knew then that it wasn't just my wild imagination and after a while I got used to the idea of living in a haunted pub and it didn't bother me. My mother has never seen her but sometimes she feels that there is someone behind her.

White Lion

THE WHITE LION IS THOUGHT TO BE THE OLDEST PUB IN ASTWOOD BANK, said to be built in 1830 but possibly earlier. An attractive white-washed building, it won the competition for the prettiest pub in the Redditch area in 1995. It was once a coaching house, with stables on the left and a number of outbuildings to the rear, one of which has been converted into a function room. The central bar is long and narrow and runs from the Bar Room on the left to a large Lounge on the right, just beyond which are the ladies' toilets. This is a village pub in every sense of the word, many of its regulars have been coming here for years, and some of them will testify to something strange apparently sneaking into the ladies' loo.

Vic is one of the old timers and he says:

I've been drinking here for 17 years, I've known all the licensees previous to this one and they all talked about this shadow. I have only seen it twice but some of the licensees have seen it lots of times. It's like a dark patch which moves across, it's difficult to describe. You look and the shadow is there but then it's gone. As well as that, I've heard the lounge door open and close many times when nobody has come in.

Bernie, another regular, adds:

There's a corner of the White Lion which always feels very cold. It gives me the creeps. There's something there, I'm sure there is. One evening in the summer of 1997 I was sitting at the bar and I turned round to see a shadow—as I was turning my head it was moving. Then nothing was there. I was very surprised, I was sure that somebody was there. It was so quick, I can't describe it, it was just a blur but it was human size. This was not a falling-on-the-floor job. I'd only had one pint of bitter.

It's not only appeared in the summer time, I've seen it in the winter too. I've seen it a few times since, usually several months apart. There is no pattern to it. I always seem to see it over the weekend, usually Saturday nights, it doesn't seem to appear during the week.

The present manager, Paul Binnell, gives more details.

The Lounge was once divided into two rooms with a corridor running between them. What is now the door to the Ladies used to be the entrance to this corridor—the lobby entrance was not there. This door makes an unusual soft click when it's opened which just catches your attention and once or twice a week I hear this door open and close yet nobody comes in. When I first came here I heard the door go, so up I gets and goes into the Lounge, surprised to find no-one there. 'Perhaps someone has come in from outside just to use the toilet' thinks I, and I stand there like an idiot. I realised after a few minutes that nobody was about. I got used to it after a few weeks and now I don't bother to go in if I hear the door open and close.

Everyone who works behind the bar hears tapping on the Lounge counter with a glass. We come in but no-one is there. I've been here three years and it's been happening all the time.

The alarms sometimes go off during the night, I come down with my baseball bat but no-one is here. I look at the security board but I know who is going to be the culprit—it is always number 5 or number 6. Number 5 is the door to the Ladies and number 6 is the next door, the first door to the Gents. There is no way these doors could blow open by accident.

We have a little Jack Russell and she won't go into the Ladies. She will make a detour round it and sometimes she stands and barks at the door.

When it's quiet and there's nobody is in the Lounge—usually about 5.30—the staff sit in the Bar. Then you can sense that something is there, more so if you are sitting on your own. It's then that the toilet door opens and a shadow moves along what was the old passageway, from the door to the Ladies to the rear door. The first time I was certain that someone was there. I heard the door go and a shadow move across, so I came into the Lounge, looked around and peered through the glass door. I couldn't believe it when I couldn't see anyone. The shadow is not very tall and you can't see any details, it's just a sheet. It moves through quite slowly like someone walking through water. Only last week a customer of ours, Bernie, said, 'Someone has just walked into the Lounge.' I had a look and no-one was there. I told him that it was our apparition. He said that he was sure he had seen someone come in and he thought we were pulling his leg.

One of the old guys who comes in at dinner times says that he can remember that a little girl, aged about 11 or 12, died here round about the 1920's in the flu epidemic.

Emma, a twenty-year old student, has been working temporarily at the White Lion since March 1996.

I would say that the first time that I experienced the ghost was the most memorable. One Sunday evening, after I had been working there for about two months, I was in the bar on my own. The landlord had disappeared to another part of the building to clear up a few odd jobs. The pub was quite quiet so I put the telly on and sat down. From where I was sitting I could see the bar area and, beyond this, the gate into the lounge. This gate is shoulder height and is near to the entrance door and the ladies' toilets. About three times in a couple of hours I saw what I thought was someone in a white T-shirt walking past the end of the bar. Because of the furnishings I could only see a torso behind the gateway. I assumed it was someone who had come in from outside and was paying a visit to the ladies' toilets. I looked in the lounge and I looked in the ladies' toilets but no-one was there. I just assumed it was me getting tired. When the landlord came back, he said, 'Have you been busy?' I said, 'No, but I keep thinking someone is coming in. I go to see who it is and there's no-one there.' He said, 'Oh, that's our ghost.' I laughed, thinking he was joking. He said, quite seriously,, 'We think it's a lady who comes in and goes to the ladies' toilets'.

This happens especially on a Sunday when the bar is quiet. I should say that I have seen it ten or more times over the past six months. It appears several times week after week, then there's a short gap—not more than a few weeks—before it turns up again. I would say that you see it three or four times during a shift from 12 to 3 o'clock.

At the end of the evening all the staff will all sit round in the bar and have a drink. Then we bring the dog in. The dog will just sit in the one spot but sometimes he will look towards the toilet door as if he has seen something, his hair will go up and he will start howling.

All the time that I'm working there I have this funny feeling that someone is watching me. It doesn't frighten me at all, I'm more intrigued than anything.

☎ 01527 892504

Mon–Sun: 1130–1530
1730–2300

Yes

Home-cooked bar meals

Yes

A Banks's pub (Wolverhampton and Dudley Breweries) with guest beers

Live music with various bands and groups, otherwise piped

ASTWOOD BANK

BEWDLEY

George Hotel

DURING THE SEVENTEENTH AND EIGHTEENTH CENTURIES,

The George Hotel was one of the most important establishments in one of England's major inland ports, and it is still a large and impressive building. Goods came from the potteries and the Black Country to be despatched on the river Severn, some to go to Bristol for export. The George Inn was the centre of social and political activities, frequented by the cream of society. In its coaching days it could stable over forty horses. It was important enough for Charles I to stay there in 1645.

The grey lady of The George is well-known. The Manager says, 'She appears every now and then and walks round one of the rooms. A few residents have seen her, usually after six pints of Burton Bitter!' She last made her presence felt at the beginning of 1996 when two guests who were sharing a room claimed that items had mysteriously moved around and that something strange had fallen off their bed in the night.

No-one knows her identity but the history of The George has been lively enough to provide a candidate or two. Engraved on one of the windows on the staircase is 'John Blome, 1777, March 4, was hanged'. Another tragedy occurred when Mr Crump, the landlord, was killed while supervising the firing of a cannon to celebrate a twenty-first birthday party on a nearby estate. Perhaps a distraught mother or widow comes to find her loved one.

☎ **01299 402117**

→ In Load Street, central Bewdley

🕐 Mon–Thu: 1200–1500
1730–2300
Fri: 1100–1500
1730–2300
Sat: All day
1200–1600
Sun: 1800–2230

🧍 Allowed in front lounge restaurant

🍴 Bar and restaurant, also coffee shop

⛩ Tables in cobbled yard under wisteria

🍺 Regular guest beers

ℹ Two-star free house with ten en suite rooms.

THE GEORGE HOTEL
Telley Bitter

I saw an elderly man
in a chair
smoking a pipe.
When I looked again
he had gone.

Victoria Arms

☎ **01386 830375**

➜ Bretforton is on B4035 about 3 miles east of Evesham

🕐 Mon–Sat: 1200–1500
              1800–2300
Sun: 1200–2230

🍴 Bar snacks and restaurant meals inc Sunday lunch

ⓘ Owned by Trent Taverns, the Victoria Arms is unusual in that it has a bowling green.

IT IS THOUGHT THAT THE VICTORIA ARMS DATES BACK TO THE SIXTEENTH CENTURY, WHEN IT WAS PROBABLY TWO LITTLE COTTAGES.

Over the years bits have been added on, small rooms have been enlarged and the old cellar has been filled in, but the original part remains at the front.

In 1989 the landlady and her eighteen-year old daughter ran the Victoria Arms between them.

The problems that we had were mostly in the flat upstairs. We would walk around and we would feel something brush past us. When we were in bed we would hear strange noises, such as a buzz of conversation coming up from downstairs. The large lounge upstairs had four radiators and on the whole it was very warm but then suddenly, on the fireplace end, you would hit an icy wall.

The gas people came to do a survey and they pulled a curiously-shaped panel out of the fireplace. Behind it was a flight of stairs leading to a bricked-up room. The pub had only just opened at lunch time one day when I saw an elderly man in a chair smoking a pipe. When I looked again he had gone. I said to my daughter, 'Where's that man gone?' and she said, 'What man?'. We searched the building but nobody was there, in any case we had only just opened so nobody could have come in. Then, when one of the locals came in, he said that for years an old man had sat in that chair smoking a pipe. He had died a few years previously.

I only saw him that once, I never saw him again.

The present licensee, Margaret, arrived in April 1997. She says that she has heard a good many rumours about the pub being haunted but she herself has never seen anything. However, she's keeping her eyes open!

Fleece Inn

THIS PICTURESQUE, HALF-TIMBERED INN HAS FEATURED IN A NUMBER OF FILMS, INCLUDING MARTIN CHUZZLEWIT, CLARISSA AND SILAS MARNER. IT WAS ORIGINALLY A MEDIEVAL FARMHOUSE, WITH THE ANIMALS SLEEPING AT ONE END AND THE FAMILY THE OTHER. THE BYRD FAMILY AND THEIR DESCENDANTS HAVE OWNED THE FLEECE SINCE THE FIFTEENTH CENTURY AND WERE FARMERS UNTIL 1848, WHEN HENRY BYRD SOLD THE LAND, CONVERTED THE HOUSE INTO A HOSTELRY AND OBTAINED A LICENCE TO SELL HOME-BREWED BEER AND CIDER. HIS GREAT GRAND-DAUGHTER, LOLA TAPLIN WAS THE LAST OF THE LINE TO MANAGE THE FLEECE WHICH SHE DID SINGLE-HANDEDLY FOR THE LAST THIRTY YEARS OF HER LIFE. SHE DIED IN 1977 AGED 83 AND LEFT IT TO THE NATIONAL TRUST ON CONDITION THAT IT WOULD CONTINUE TO BE RUN AS AN UNSPOILT COUNTRY PUB. AND SO IT HAS REMAINED, UNTOUCHED BY TIME, WITH THE FAMILY FURNITURE AND ORNAMENTS STILL IN PLACE. TO WALK INTO THE FLEECE IS TO STEP STRAIGHT INTO THE PAST. MISS TAPLIN PAINTED WHITE CIRCLES ROUND THE HEARTH TO STOP THE WITCHES COMING DOWN THE CHIMNEY AND INTO THE ROOM, AND ALL THE CRACKS UNDER THE TABLES WERE PAINTED WHITE TO STOP THE WITCHES COMING UP. THESE WHITE LINES WERE FREQUENTLY RENEWED AND CAN STILL BE SEEN.

Miss Taplin was a formidable lady and ruled the inn with a rod of iron. Swearing and disorderly behaviour was not allowed. The locals remember a time when an American asked for ice and she told him in no uncertain times that he only got ice when it snowed. They also remember the high-spirited gentleman who burst into song and was consequently banned. Peter Holden recalls pulling a chocolate bar out of his pocket while in the Fleece, when he was told in no uncertain terms to leave the premises.

Miss Taplin would never allow food to be eaten on the premises. Some time after she had passed away, the builders arrived and they, of course, ate their sandwiches in the disused pub. To their surprise, they found that their lunch boxes were often turned upside down and the sandwiches scattered about.

The present licensee, Norman, says that he tries to run the pub almost exactly as Miss Taplin would have wished.

I'm not quite as strict but I won't have bad language in here and I won't have people being heavy handed with the furniture. Lola was very particular where she had her furniture and I try to put everything back as Lola would have done, but sometimes it does get moved. The strange thing is, that when something is out of place, I can hear furniture moving during the night. I come down and put all the lights on but there's nobody here. I have the dog with me and she growls when I come into the Brewhouse.

All kinds of strange things happen here. I've been here since 1981 and the first thing I noticed was that when I came into the Brew-house after hours to put out the lights, the hackles of my old dog used to rise. At times I hear a movement, but when I go to investigate, nobody is there. A lot of people who come into the pub say that there is a presence here. I never get that feeling myself, but sometimes, when I'm here on my own, I feel that someone is watching me. I used to be a non-believer but now I have an open mind.

The clock in the Brewhouse regularly stopped at 3 o'clock in the morning. Quite by chance I discovered that Lola died at about that time. She fell down in the passage and broke her hip then pneumonia set in.

The alarm system in the Pewter room would go off for no reason. Her rocking chair was beneath the alarm so I moved it and I haven't had any trouble since. I'm not saying that the rocking of the chair caused the alarm to go off, I'm just saying that I don't know what the explanation could be.

Whenever we put white flowers on the table near the window of the Brewhouse, they have dropped by the next day. My wife noticed it first. When she uses coloured flowers, they last for a week or more. Then we heard from some of our regulars that Lola always used to have white flowers on that table. We have tried using different types of flower but it's always the white ones that wilt quickly.

When Lola was alive, the front of the pub used to have a big grape-vine. When she died, the vine did too. There have been three or four landlords before me and they have all had a go at planting a vine but it died. The vine that I planted has taken, I look upon this as a symbol that she is looking down on the running of the pub and I am doing it the way that she wanted.

☎ **01386 831173**

	Mon–Sat:	1100–1500
		1800–2300
	Sun:	1100–1500
		1800–2230

Yes

Yes (garden)

Owned by the National Trust. Morris dancing takes place three or four times a year. Featured in *Pub Walks in Worcestershire* and mentioned in the *Good Pub Guide*. Awarded two stars.

BRETFORTON

☎ 01527 579007

→ Leave the M5 at junction
5 and join the A38
signposted Bromsgrove.
The first traffic island is
the turning for Webb's
Garden Centre, carry
straight on. At the
second roundabout,
bear left, again sign-
posted Bromsgrove.
After half a mile you will
come to Grafton Lane
which is first on the left

🏕 26 acres of grounds
including a two-acre
lake suitable for coarse
fishing

ⓘ The hotel is owned and
managed by the Morris
family. John Morris is
now the Lord of Grafton.
Awards: AA two star,
member of the Master
Chefs Institute and in
the Good Hotel guide

it
started to
swirl in
two spirals,
perfect circles,
side by
side

Grafton Manor Hotel

THIS GRACEFUL TUDOR MANOR HOUSE WAS ORIGINALLY THE HOME OF THE GRAFTON FAMILY BUT CAME INTO THE HANDS OF SIR HUMPHREY STAFFORD IN 1449. HE WAS EXECUTED FOR TREASON EARLY IN THE REIGN OF HENRY VII. IN 1555 IT PASSED INTO THE HANDS OF JOHN TALBOT, A RELATIVE OF THE EARL OF SHREWSBURY, WHO SPENT MOST OF HIS LIFE EITHER IN PRISON OR UNDER CURFEW FOR HIS RELIGIOUS BELIEFS. HE MANAGED TO REBUILD THE HOUSE IN 1567, PUTTING THE INSCRIPTION OVER THE PORCH DOOR:

> Plenty and grace bide in this place
> While every man is placed in his degree
> there is both peace and unity
> Solomon said there is none accord
> when every man would be a lord.

(modern translation)

It remains to this day, despite a severe fire in 1710. The house was extensively rebuilt in the 1860s and is now a hotel.

Jon Bond now lives and farms in Devon, but the following incident occurred in the mid 1980's, when he lived in Grafton Cottage which is right beside the existing fishponds. He farmed the local fields and had working dogs which he kept in kennels outside.

The people who lived next door, Steve and Sue, said to me one morning, 'Did you hear all the commotion last night at about three-thirty? Your dogs were going absolutely mental! We looked out of the window and somebody dressed in white was walking across the field next to the pond.'

They thought it could have been one of the cooks from Grafton Manor Hotel. I knew Simon Morris, the son of the manager and I asked him if this was possible but he said that nobody would be out at that time in the morning. I gave this bit of information to my neighbours and they told me that they hadn't seen the white figure very clearly as it had been dark. However, saying that, the night was clear, the figure was no more than 100 yards away and they had watched it walk across the field for several minutes. They had got the impression that it was a guy. That was the end of it as far as I was concerned.

The next night I was woken up by the dogs going absolutely mental. I looked at my watch and the time was half past three. I went to the window and looked out, the night was clear and starry. I stood there for several minutes but I couldn't see anything. I had a word with my neighbours the next day but they hadn't even heard the dogs barking.

I had heard tales of the grey lady of Grafton. I was told that she had been going past the pool in a horse-drawn cart when the cart overturned and she was drowned. It wouldn't surprise me to learn that the pool was originally much larger than it is now as the fishpond is below the level of the road and the field next to it has a series of little duckponds.

This second story is taken from *Haunted Worcestershire*.

As an energetic young man Carl Mills is not usually interested in old mansions but the hot summer of 1995 found him lounging indoors, idly flipping through the pages of a local history book. A description of Grafton Manor caught his eye and therefore when, late one evening a few days later, he and three friends were wondering where they could go, Carl made a suggestion.

We decided to go for a midnight walk, somewhere dark, mysterious, and spooky so I suggested Grafton Manor pool. There was Clare, and two friends of ours, John and Karen. We drove to the Manor house and were able to park near to the pool.

We came to the edge of the pool and saw the crossed trees where a lady is supposed to have drowned herself. John and Karen were in front as we continued walking towards the manor. We paused and were looking across to the bridge when we noticed, through a gap in the hedge on our left, a patch of fog on the bank. It was most peculiar fog and it was just in that one patch. It kept rolling off the bank and dropping into the water. Suddenly it came towards us and when it was ten or fifteen feet away it started to swirl in two spirals, perfect circles, side by side, both going in opposite directions, rather like candy floss. When it was about 10 or 15 feet away the shape began to change and it began to assume a human form. It went up and up until it was about six feet tall and at the same time it narrowed, so that it was very thin. The top part seemed to divide into two peaks like arms. When it came to within six feet of us we decided to retreat to the car and drive back to the entrance gates.

Grafton Manor Pool is privately owned and as it is surrounded by a thick hedge, very difficult to see from the road. A visit to the pool without first visiting the hotel is not recommended.

BROMSGROVE

Ye Olde Black Cross

THE MAIN ROAD FROM REDDITCH TO KIDDERMINSTER ONCE CROSSED THE WORCESTER ROAD OUTSIDE THE BLACK CROSS INN AND AT THESE CROSS ROADS, SAY THE LOCALS, STOOD A GIBBET USED FOR HANGING SHEEP STEALERS. THIS IS HOW THE BLACK CROSS CAME BY ITS NAME.

In a town which is renowned for its ancient hostelries, the Black Cross building is the oldest. By 1651 it had been in existence for many years and part of the building was a small forge. This was the year in which the bloody battle of Worcester took place, when the largely Scottish army of Charles Stuart fought the Parliamentarians. Charles Stuart, who later became Charles II, narrowly escaped from the battle and fled for his life. He was given a horse at Worcester but at Bromsgrove it threw a shoe.

Several historians have identified the forge which reshod the horse as the one at the Black Cross. King Charles later wrote:

'As I was holding my horse's foot I asked the smith the news… He answered that he did not hear that rogue, Charles Stuart, was taken… some of the others, he said, were taken but not Charles Stuart. I told him that if that rogue were taken he deserved to be hanged more than all the rest for bringing in the Scots, upon which he said I spoke like an honest man, and so we parted.'

Reg and Edith Jackson Cox were the owners and licensees of the Black Cross from 1970 to 1983. He says:

As a result of its history there were several visitations, in fact a soldier or Royalist was seen many times before we took over.

About five years after we arrived a girl who was our Head Buyer went to the toilet down a long passage and she came back saying she had seen a ghost. She said it was a soldier in a long cloak and a broad-rimmed hat. It didn't try to grab her or anything—it didn't budge, it just stood there. Whether it was a hallucination or not I don't know but she was convinced she had seen something.

We had an assistant manager sleeping in one of the upstairs rooms. I came in one day and he said, 'I'm not prepared to sleep there again'. He told me that he was in bed when this figure appeared and walked through the door. I told him he had had too much to drink but he was adamant. He said, 'I'm telling you I'm not going up there again'. His description was just the same as the Head Buyer's. It was really too much of a coincidence.

A few years later my wife had an accident in Weston-super-Mare and was in hospital for some time.

She eventually came home to sleep at the Black Cross in the bedroom just above the bar, which goes back to the 1640's. It was the original house before it became a pub, when it was a one up one down cottage. There were all kinds of weird noises and creaks there. One evening, I was sitting in the lounge of the pub when I heard a loud bump on the floor. I thought my wife had fallen out of bed.

I rushed upstairs and found her sitting up in bed. I asked her, 'Have you stepped out of bed? I heard a thump'. She said that she had not moved and added 'I did hear some footsteps but I thought it was one of the staff'. Nobody had been up there at all. It seems to me quite doubtful that it was someone in our time at all.

Mr Albrighton, the present manager, adds:

Our ghost has been very active during the past six months. My wife has been touched five times on the back and bum and two members of staff have been touched (honest!). We have never seen anything, only felt someone's presence.

The old forge is now the bottle store and you can still see the rings in the wall where the horses were tied up, King Charles' horse among them.

 01527 870326

 In central Bromsgrove, at the start of the Worcester Road, by the zebra crossing

Mon–Fri: 1200–1500
         1730–2300
Sat: 1100–2300
Sun: 1200–2230

 Allowed for dining

 Home-cooked bar snacks during lunchtimes and most evenings

 Yes

 Banks' beers, Marstons' and four special lagers

ⓘ Owned by the Wolver-hampton and Dudley Breweries. Accommodation: Four en suite rooms. Large car park and a juke box.

Shoulder *of* Mutton Inn

IN THE CENTRE OF BROMSGROVE IS A STATUE TO THE POET, ALFRED HOUSMAN, WHO LIVED AT
Perry Hall (at the start of the Kidderminster Road) until he was twelve. Nearby, in Saint John's Street, is the Shoulder of Mutton Inn.
Housman's father was a well-known character here, he would often call in for a drink and the landlord provided Perry Hall with beer and
sherry. He would let the landlord know when further supplies were needed by throwing stones on the tin roof of an adjoining outbuilding.

The Shoulder of Mutton is probably about four hundred years old and was once a coaching inn although there is now very little of
the original building left. It used to be the custom to allow regulars a free meal occasionally, perhaps on a Sunday and on Saint's days,
and pubs took their name from the meal offered, hence its name.

Maureen Lines was landlady of the Shoulder of Mutton from 1975 until she moved to the Red Lion in Astwood Bank in 1994.

**There was definitely a ghost there; we had all kinds of problems. Stuff would be moved, for example, we would find
saucepans in places that we knew we hadn't put them. Clothes used to be moved from one wardrobe to another, I would find
my husband's clothes in my wardrobe and he would find mine in his.**

ONE TUESDAY EVENING
AT ABOUT 8.30,
I WAS SITTING
WITH ONE OF OUR REGULARS WHEN
SUDDENLY THE DOOR **BURST OPEN** AND ALL THE
PICTURES BEGAN **SWINGING** AND JERKING ABOUT.
I'VE NEVER SEEN ANYTHING LIKE IT.
I RAN OUTSIDE
BUT THERE WAS NO WIND
AND NO-ONE WAS THERE.

I had been working so hard one night that I had dropped off to sleep on the sofa in the Lounge. I was woken up at
about 5.30 am by a door slamming—they have ball catches in the Shoulder of Mutton. I woke up to see the ghost of the
grey lady coming from the kitchen into the lounge. She was young, tall and slim, in a long dress, very misty and all slatey
grey. I can see her now.

I didn't wait to see where she went. I jumped up and ran into the bedroom

☎ **01527 574156**

→ 16 St John Street,
Bromsgrove centre,
opposite market car park

⊘ Mon–Sat: 1100–1500
1700–2300
Sun: 1200–1500

🍴 Home-cooked meals
served in a small
restaurant

🪑 Beer garden

🍺 The Shoulder of Mutton's
strength lies in its range
of beers. It offers
traditional 6X Wadworth,
Flowers IPA,
Boddington's Gold, John
Smith's Smooth and too
many others to list

ⓘ Owned by Trent Taverns
(Whitbread).

 **01527 550050**

Off the Bromsgrove/
Redditch highway—
follow the signs to
Blakenhurst and the
other HM establishments
and it's almost opposite
the entrance

 Mon–Sat: 1100–2300
Sun: 1200–2300

Children's play area
(Wacky Warehouse)
Open from 1100–2000

 Mainly restaurant meals
with waitress service

Garden with play area

Owned by Allied Domeq
Leisure

We could see
them shattering
before our eyes

BROMSGROVE TARDEBIGGE

the Tardebigge

THE TARDEBIGGE WAS BUILT AS A VILLAGE HALL BY THE EARL

of Plymouth who lived in Hewell Grange nearby. Unfortunately, the locals have not had much of an opportunity to enjoy their gift. It was used as a hospital for servicemen during the first world war then later, two Earls of Plymouth died soon after each other and as the villagers could not prove that the hall belonged to them, the Tardebigge was sold in 1946 to help offset the heavy death duties.

The Tardebigge has had the reputation of being haunted for many years. When Gerald Ludden took over in 1988, his children came home from school crying because the other children had told them that they were going to live in a haunted house. As it happened, Gerald had been puzzled that first day by a curious incident, told here by Barbara, the Assistant Manager.

The top shelf of the bar is full of two-pint tankards, and just on that day they kept splitting down the middle. We could see them shattering before our eyes with no-one anywhere near them. There was no regular pattern, sometimes two would split together, sometimes three. Sometimes we would go for an hour or even two without a breakage. These tankards have thick bases, you can drop them on the floor and they don't break, yet they were shattering for no apparent reason. It was very weird.

Barbara had other tales to tell.

One of my tasks is to write out the table plans for large functions. I was doing this one lovely sunny afternoon in June last year, kneeling on the floor. The sun was streaming through the windows and the atmosphere was not at all eerie. Suddenly, I felt someone come up behind me and I felt a tap on my shoulder. I turned round to see who it was, and to my surprise no-one was there.

A few years ago we had a great strapping bloke, John, working behind the bar. He was at least six feet six inches tall. One day he came up from the cellar looking ashen. He said he had heard someone sneezing down there but when he went to see who it was the cellar was empty.

We have problems with our names being called. A young lady's voice comes from behind a dumb waiter which we keep just in front of the false doors. I've only heard it twice because I don't normally work in the function room but the waitresses often hear it. Two waitresses here recently, Samantha and Debbie, found it a real nuisance. They kept saying to each other 'What do you want?' and 'Did you call me?' and getting very confused.

The Restaurant Supervisor, Pauline, had experienced other incidents.

I have been having problems in the main lounge. For several weeks in the spring of 1991, I had been helping out with the cleaning, and I kept putting my duster down but when I went to pick it up I found that it had moved, sometimes to another chair or table. Then early one morning, I was hoovering round when I heard this fella laughing just behind me. I switched the vacuum off and turned round to see who it was, but no-one was there. However, the liquid polish had been knocked over and was trickling across the table. I found the incident so weird that I refused to go into the main lounge each morning until several staff had arrived.

A few months later we found a cleaner, Rose, and exactly the same thing happened to her. First of all her dusters kept moving around, then she heard this bloke laugh behind her - no-one was there but the liquid polish had been knocked over. She left after a week.

A couple of long-term customers live across the road and they say that about twenty years ago, one of our regulars had a passion for practical jokes and, before he died, he spent all his time playing jokes on people. Several times recently they are certain that they have seen him sitting in the raised area.

Gerald Ludden, the manager, added:

We had a problem with the burglar alarm which kept going off for absolutely no reason. It still goes off now every couple of months and no-one has any idea why. Then there was this strange sensation which I felt whenever I walked across the function room. It's difficult to describe, it was a kind of chill in the air which made me shudder although I wasn't physically cold.

A few years ago a lady who had heard that the place was haunted asked if she could have a look round to try and locate the ghost. Not knowing that the Tardebigge was used as a hospital during the First World War, she told me that we have a presence here, a nurse by the name of Emily. She is a benign presence and there is no need to be afraid of her.

You might think that, since the function room is supposed to be haunted, I would be afraid to go in there. Not a bit of it: I go in every evening and never even bother to switch the lights on. The feeling that there is someone with me is so strong that as I come out I always say, 'Goodnight Em!'.

Rock Tavern

THIS INN CAPTURED THE IMAGINATION OF A POPULAR VICTORIAN NOVELIST, SABINE BARING-GOULD. Although his novel *The Bladys of the Stewponey* begins in the Stewponey Inn, the plot revolves chiefly around 'The Rock Tavern' and it is here that he sets his most dramatic scenes.

Standing high above the river Stour the tavern is, in Baring-Gould's words:

…constructed against a face of rock, which served as an inner wall, and this face was dug into it to form recesses for shelves, and pierced by a door that probably gave access to the cellar.

Through this door are other rooms cut into the rock and these, in the past, have been used as hideouts by highwaymen. Baring-Gould explains why the area was infested with them. The proximity of the waterways and the main roads meant that travellers going north, south, east or west passed through the district. He describes the county boundaries 'as having gone through extraordinary dislocation' and continues:

Nothing was more easy for one who desired to throw out his pursuers, armed with a warrant signed by the magistrate of one county, than to pass into the next, and if further pursued by legal process there, to step into a third. …But this was not all. The geological structure of the country favoured them. Wherever a cliff, great or small, presented its escarpment, there the soft sandstone was scooped out into labyrinths of chambers, in which families dwelt, who in not a few instances were in league with the land pirates. The plunder could anywhere be safely and easily concealed, and the plunderers could pass through subterranean passages out of one county into another and so elude pursuit.

Both the Stewponey and the Rock Tavern have, say the locals, had the reputation of being in league with highwaymen.

The Bladys of the Stewponey begins in the early 1700s when the landlord decides to marry off his beautiful daughter, commonly known as Bla, to the winner of a game of bowls (which becomes a wrestling match). Alas for poor Bla, of the three main suitors, one turns out to be the Shrewsbury executioner and another a gentleman highwayman. The executioner wins her hand but Bla becomes ill on the journey to his home and is taken to the Rock Tavern. The licensee's daughter, Nan, becomes her best friend and rescues her from many an adventure. In a final dramatic conclusion, the highwayman (who has been betrothed to Nan) is poisoned at the Rock Tavern by the elderly female licensee, Nan's mother.

Although the Rock Tavern has changed its name twice, being known as 'The Britannia' before 1825 and more recently as 'The Portelet Inn', there is no doubt from the many references in the text that this is the inn referred to.

The locals are agreed that sometime in the past a terrible murder was committed there. Some say that a mother murdered her daughter, others that it was a wife who stabbed her husband. Perhaps it was a mother who stabbed her daughter's lover, and Baring-Gould uses it in his novel. It is agreed that the victim collapsed on the step which leads from the far end of the bar into a little room which was once the loo and now used to store odds and ends such as the dart board.

The present licensees, Marlene and Jeff, arrived in July 1994, and Marlene tells the following story:

One evening, all the family were sitting round a table at the far end with my sister-in-law in front of the doorway to the store room. All of a sudden she got up and said, 'Oh!'. She told us that somebody had just run his fingers down the back of her neck. It makes me feel cold to think of it, but I made a joke of it. I said, 'Well, Pauline, you are blocking the doorway and perhaps the ghost wants to get out!'

I had heard that there was a murder in that corner and that the place was supposed to be haunted but I didn't actually take a lot of notice. However, other strange things have happened. One evening, five of us were sitting round a table, each with a drink, then one of the ladies got up to get another round and one of gentlemen went off to the loo so that there were just three of us left sitting there, just talking. Suddenly, one of the glasses jumped up and tipped over, emptying its contents on to the floor. It was so peculiar that we couldn't believe it so we pretended not to notice and carried on talking. Everyone knew what they had seen and wondered if anyone else had seen it. Then we looked at each other, stopped talking and said, 'Did you see that?'.

The previous licensees were Richard and Lisa Hunter; they reported to the local press that the tables and chairs moved of their own accord, sometimes in front of customers. So, who is responsible for the haunting? Is it the murderer or his victim? Or is it an executed highwayman who returns to take refuge in those caves which sheltered him during his lifetime?

☎ **01562 850416**

→ Caunsell is about three miles north of Kidderminster and is signposted from the A449. The Rock Tavern is about a quarter of a mile from the main road

🕐 Wed–Sat
and Mon: 1200–2300
Tues: 1600–2300
Sun: 1200–1500
             1900–2230

👤 Allowed on small patio area adjacent to road

🍴 Bar snacks

🍺 Marsden's bitter and Pedigree, Banks's mild, cider, guest ale and a variety of lagers

ⓘ Social evenings once a month, especially during the summer when the caravan site by the river down below is in full swing, they include Morris dancers, quiz nights, live music, race nights for charity and a bonfire night with Black Country food such as groaty dick.

CAUNSELL NEAR KIDDERMINSTER

Mug House

THE OLD MUG HOUSE IS NEXT TO THE CHURCH AND IS THE ONLY PUBLIC HOUSE IN THE COUNTRY TO STAND ON CONSECRATED GROUND. THE CHURCH WAS REBUILT IN THE FIFTEENTH CENTURY AND THE PUB WAS PROBABLY ERECTED ABOUT THE SAME TIME. IT HAS SUCH A REPUTATION FOR BEING HAUNTED THAT THE LANDLORD HAS FREQUENT REQUESTS FROM GHOST HUNTERS ASKING IF THEY CAN STAY THE NIGHT, WHICH HE HAS TO REFUSE AS HE DOES NOT PROVIDE OVERNIGHT ACCOMMODATION. BILL GWILLAM, IN Old Worcestershire Inns, STATES THAT TRADITIONALLY THE GHOST WALKS TO THE DOOR, CRIES 'BEWARE', THEN GOES INTO THE CHURCH TO PLAY THE ORGAN.

Wally Trow was landlord from 1938 to 1982 but he's sceptical about the ghost. However, he admits that he heard many an inexplicable noise and that he had problems in the cellar where his mallet, which he used to bang the taps in, was mysteriously moved about. He also recalls that 30 or 40 years ago a Curate by the name of Marks had seen a white mist, which had assumed a human form, inside the church. Mr Marks was a most responsible person, he had once been secretary to Sir Winston Churchill but had decided to enter the ministry late in life.

Wally Trow's wife takes the ghost stories more seriously.

The Old Mug House was a creepy place. It was dark and full of strange noises. When we lay in bed at night we could sometimes hear the glasses rattling for no reason at all. We often heard strange footsteps. Many times I heard someone go downstairs in the night so I got out of bed to see who it was but no-one was there. I remember one afternoon when I definitely heard someone go in the house and up the stairs, I rushed to the stair door and locked it. I thought, 'Well, whoever it is, I've got them now' but when Wally and I went upstairs to see who it was, no-one was there.

Sometimes things went missing but with two children we didn't think much of it. I remember something strange, though, which happened over and over again. When we went to bed at night we put a plate of biscuits on the side in case one of the children got up in the night, but they didn't get up and some mornings the biscuits had gone. We put it down to mice but there were never any crumbs or droppings and other bits and pieces of food were never touched.

John Adkins has been landlord since the summer of 1989. He and his wife, Judy, were also sceptical about ghosts when they first moved but they have had so many strange experiences that they are beginning to change their minds. John takes up the narrative:

The first weird event happened late one Sunday afternoon, about three months after we had moved in. The bar was closed and we were sitting round a table in the lounge, eating a meal with about eight friends and neighbours when suddenly, from behind the bar, came an enormous crash. We rushed to the bar to find half-a-dozen glasses which had been kept on a low shelf had smashed to the floor with such force that they had been reduced to small particles like ground glass. It was so weird that our friends, who were staying in the cottage next door, said 'We're not stopping here any longer!', threw their luggage in their car and drove back to London.

About six weeks later it happened again. Colin, the barman, and Joanne, a niece who was staying temporarily to help, were leaning against one end of the bar early one evening, having a chat, when there was a loud crash. Several glasses had fallen to the floor and were completely shattered into such small pieces it was impossible to tell how many had been broken. Colin and Joanne were quite amazed because there was absolutely no reason for it, in fact Joanne was quite frightened.

From the first day that we arrived our dog, an American spaniel, began howling and it had never howled before. Eventually we realised that he only howls when he is in the kitchen. The flap to the cellar is in the kitchen and it's in the cellar that many strange things have occurred.

I'm the only person to go down the cellars and one night I went down and turned the barrels on, then I came upstairs and served a glass of cider. Judy went to serve a second glass but no cider came out, then I told her that it couldn't have because I'd only just checked the barrel. She said, 'The cider's run out!' and I told her that it couldn't have because I'd only just checked the barrel. I decided I would have to go down the cellar again to see what was wrong so down I went and checked the piping. Then I noticed that the electric motor was switched off. I could not believe it. This has to be turned off manually with a switch and there is no way it could have been done by accident. The same thing happened again a few months later, then again, a few months after that.

Only last Saturday night something weird happened in the cellar. At four o'clock in the morning the dog began howling and this set the other dog off. The next morning I went down the cellar and I could hardly believe my eyes. All round the walls of the cellar are steps called stillages which are about a foot wide and between two and three feet in length for the barrels of beer to rest on so that they are not standing on the floor. Somehow, a barrel of beer, which takes two men to lift, had managed to remove itself from the stillage, complete with pipes and other fittings, and was resting on the floor.

Several glasses had fallen to the floor and were

COMPLETELY
SHATTERED
INTO SUCH SMALL PIECES it was impossible to tell how many had been broken.

The most frightening incident occurred early in 1991. This convinced me that there is something spooky about this place. Judy and I were both woken up by the noise of a door opening at half-past one in the morning. Now, when you live in an old house you get used to certain noises and we knew that it was the door of the Smoking Room. It's old and heavy and first you have to turn back the heavy door handle, then drag the door open. Next the door was closed with a loud bang. The door has a heavy bolt on the corridor side and the room contains an infra-red security device so that when the door opens, the alarm is set off. We lay there, expecting the alarm to go off but nothing happened. Again the door noisily opened and closed, followed by a rest of about 15 seconds, then it happened again. Judy said to me, 'What are you going to do about it?' I said 'Nothing, I'm just stopping here where I am!'. I was petrified, although I suppose if the alarms had gone off I would have gone downstairs. In all the door opened and banged shut six times. When we got up the next morning we found that the door was still bolted. We had the security system checked and there was nothing wrong with it.

Judy added that she would not sleep in the house alone.

On the rare occasions that my husband has to go away, my son comes to stay with me. If I was here alone and the dogs began howling I just wouldn't be able to cope. Our cleaner will never work on her own, she can hear someone moving about upstairs when she knows that nobody is there. Our barman won't stay on his own either, he hears the rattling of drawers in empty rooms and the opening and closing of doors.

CLAINES

the Vine

THE VINE IS SITUATED ON THE EDGE OF THE CLENT HILLS AND FRONTS ON TO A WINDING COUNTRY ROAD. A HEALTHY STREAM RUNS THROUGH ITS GARDEN, FED BY THE NATURAL SPRINGS OF THE HILLS.

The sign of the vine goes back to the fourteenth century when a wreath of hops at the end of a hop pole showed that beer was for sale. The pub was probably originally an old mill, known to exist in 1522. The first licensee, George Haines, took over in 1836. As an inn, the Vine was permitted to stay open as long as a bed was empty, offering basic accommodation, simple food, home-brewed ale and stabling to the lawful traveller.

David Whitehouse is now bar manager of the pub, together with his fiancée, Michelle, whose father has been licensee for 25 years. Michelle has always known that the pub was haunted, almost from the time she came to live there at the age of five. One evening, she and her sister were upstairs asleep and a baby sitter was looking after them. The locals had all gone home and the pub was closed. The baby sitter was sitting in the bar in front of the old open fire when she heard footsteps upstairs. She thought one of the girls must have got out of bed and went upstairs to see, but they were both fast asleep. This happened three times. On the fourth time the baby sitter realised that there was nothing above the bar, the girls' bedrooms were in another part of the building. She was immensely scared and spent the rest of the evening upstairs with the girls.

David says that both the cleaners feel a presence here and sometimes they accuse him of creeping up on them when he hasn't been here. At other times they see something out of the corner of their eye. He continues:

When something strange happens, it always seems to be in the old part of the pub, not in the newer extension. The bar and a short passageway are in the old part, so is the corridor from the bedroom to the family living room. The floor here is very uneven, it goes up and down. One Tuesday night recently at about 9.15, Michelle walked along this corridor and opened the living room door. She found herself being pushed back out of the living room, nothing violent, quite a gentle push but enough to put her on her backside.

I had gone out and when I came back I could tell that something was the matter but she was so surprised that it was some time before she could tell me what had happened.

Another incident only happened about three weeks back (beginning of October 1997). I was in the bar and Michelle was in the kitchen. She came through this short corridor to me and said, 'Have you just walked up the corridor?' I said that I had been in the bar serving. She said that she had just seen a man had come along the corridor. When she saw him he had turned back so she only saw his back view and she thought it was me.

I heard about a further incident a few weeks ago when Michelle's father's friend and I were sitting talking in the bar late one night. She said, 'I haven't told you this before, but about eighteen months ago I saw a woman on the landing'. She told me that this woman was wearing a long flowing dress which looked as if it belonged to the eighteenth century. It was so vivid that she said, 'Excuse me' as she went past.

Then she suddenly realised that nobody should have been there. She turned round and the woman had gone.

The only time I have seen anything unusual was when I was bottling up one morning. I got a glimpse of a woman's reflection in the glass of the cigar cases at the rear of the bar and I saw that this woman went into the other bar. Now, the layout of the place is such that I can go from one bar to another through a short passageway without having to go through the public area. I walked round the corner to serve this woman through the side passage and no-one was there. The cleaner was in the bar and I asked her where the woman had gone. She said that she hadn't seen anyone. I checked the toilets and the car park but nobody was around. When I thought about it afterwards, the woman had looked a bit strange; although I only saw her head and shoulders I could see that she had her hair in an old-fashioned bun. It brings tingles to my spine now when I think about it.

☎ **01562 882491**

→ In Vine Lane, Upper Clent. Leave the M5 at junction 3. Take the A456, turn left at the third island and right at the T-junction up a narrow lane. Or, leave the M5 at junction 4, take the A491, watch for the road signposted Clent on the left, turn first right at the cross-roads and carry on past the Church.

Mon–Sat:
Summer: 1100–1500
                1800–2300
Winter: 1100–1500
                1900–2230
Sun: 1200–1500
                1900–2230

Allowed if under supervision

Home-cooked bar meals and snacks (including Balti) every lunch-time and evening

Garden and patio, both set out with chairs and tables

Caffery's Irish Ale is available in the bar

A very popular Bass pub. Juke box ('not modern' says the manager). Featured in *Pub Walks in Worcestershire*

☎ **01886 812617**

➔ On the B4204 halfway
between Worcester and
Tenbury Wells

🕐 Mon–Sun:
1200–1500
1800–2300
Food: 1200–1400
1830–2130

🧑 Yes

🍴 For fifteen years a
chef-award winning
restaurant

🎪 Yes

🍺 Guest ales,
Boddingtons/Guiness

ⓘ Two rooms are available
for accommodation.
Special recommend-
ations include an AA
rosette. The landlord
states, 'This is a twelfth
century family-run inn
with a relaxed atmos-
phere that serves great
food—more than just
pub grub'.

Lion Inn

CLIFTON-ON-TEME IS ONE OF the prettiest villages in Worcestershire, so much so that Clifton has been designated a conservation area. The church, with its 13th century tower, has survived the centuries, so has the village green, although the original oak in the centre of the green has now been replaced by a chestnut tree. Important legal matters were often discussed and settled under this tree because of its proximity to the Lion Inn. Built in 1157, the Lion was originally a manor house but it was also used as a court and as a Guildhall where merchants, who had come to the weekly market, bought and sold their wares. The coat of arms of the Lords of the Manor (the Jeffreys of Ham Castle) was a lion rampant, hence its name. The chimney stack on the outside wall dates from medieval times. Originally, the Lion had an open fire in the centre of the room and the fireplace is still in the same position, standing centrally in a large room which has a dining area at one end and a bar at the other.

This is not only the prettiest of villages, it also seems to be one of the most haunted. The apparitions listed in the *Worcestershire Village Book* include phantom horses, a white lady bending over a baby's cot, a nurse from the civil war, and ghostly soldiers in the steep woods leading down to the Teme. One warm summer morning recently just as dawn was breaking several residents heard a horse and cart trundling past their open windows and a terrified woman crying out 'People, people!'. The licensee of the Lion Inn admits, 'A lot of people have ghosts in the houses around here, it's a very old village'.

Not surprisingly, the Lion Inn also has a ghost. One of the waiters tells the story that when he first began working there as a teenager in about 1982, he went to put a glass on the table and he felt a hand. Nothing was visible but he was unable to put the glass in that spot.

The present licensee, Richard, only moved to the Lion at the end of 1996, but already he and his wife have experienced their strange visitor. Richard says:

When we first came here our dog used to absolutely spare. It really sensed something, it used to go nuts. We would leave the doors open but we still had to go down in the night because he was barking his head off.

I have heard several accounts of the ghost and they all seem to be of the same person, there is no deviation. The only slightly worrying thing is that when we first moved here my five-year old daughter had terrible nightmares. One night when we went into her she seemed to be looking at something and pushing it away, shouting, 'Get away, get away!'. However, it doesn't bother me at all. It's only seen in the Lounge and whatever-it-is, is quite friendly.

Richard's wife, Jane, is reluctant to talk about their strange guest and needs some persuasion to give her experiences.

I feel as if I am betraying him by talking about him. I just get the feeling that he doesn't want everyone to know he's there. It's as if he says to me, 'I'm only passing through from one room to another'. He knows I am there but he doesn't look at me. I feel that he's a very nice person and I don't want to upset him. If I met him face to face perhaps I would be scared, but I know that he is just passing through.

I have seen him twice, both times about midnight after we had just cleared up. I had only been here two days and I was on my own in the Lounge when I saw this man walk across the room from one door and disappear on the other side of the open fireplace. He was about 55, grey and getting a bit thin on top and he walked very slowly. He looked like a gardener, with a shirt and waistcoat, and loose-fitting trousers. His clothes were not too old, but not modern. He was not solid, but again, I couldn't see things through him. He was only there for a second or two before he disappeared round the back of the fireplace. I couldn't see round the fireplace so I assumed there was a fire exit there but when I went to investigate there was only a window so he must have walked through the wall. I went upstairs and said to my husband, 'A man has just walked through the wall!'. Afterwards, everyone said to me, 'Don't you know about the ghost?'.

The second time I saw him I was talking to my husband and John, the Barman, in the Lounge. I looked over John's shoulder and I saw the apparition walking across the room. I think I gave a faint smile, because John said, 'You have seen the ghost again, haven't you?'.

Only a night or two ago I was on my own when someone followed me up the stairs. When I got into bed, I said to my husband, 'You've always wanted to see the ghost and I know that whatever I saw is very close'. As I said it, my daughter in the next room started to sleep talk and the toilet seat went up and down twice. Then everything went still. It was really strange and my husband was very impressed.

This is a beautiful old house, I feel that I'm very privileged to live here and I enjoy sharing it with people.

01905 774233
/774728

 Situated opposite the
Norbury Theatre in Friar
Street

 Mon–Sat: 1130–1500
1730–2300
Sun: 1230–1500

 Good bar and restaurant
meals

Guest beers

 An interesting olde
worlde building
sensitively converted
into restaurant

Old Cock Inn

THE FAR END OF FRIAR STREET, WHICH IS NOW A DEAD END, HAS MANY GHOSTS.

Peter Mellor testifies to the one at the Norbury Theatre and some of the people living in Norbury House have had strange experiences. It is not surprising that this area is haunted, as it is said to have suffered heavily during the civil war. In 1642, the Roundheads ordered bailiffs and officers of Droitwich to keep a magazine of arms at Droitwich. Sometime later, the Cavaliers occupied the church of St Nicholas which once stood at the end of Friar Street. The Roundheads were encamped on higher ground at Dodderhill and were able to fire their canons into Friar Street. The church was totally destroyed but the villagers managed to rescue three windows which were incorporated into the rebuilding of The Old Cock Inn. They can still be seen, together with a wonderful original fireplace and a wealth of exposed beams.

The stone carving above the front entrance is thought to be that of the notorious Judge Jeffries (1648-89). He was the youngest ever Lord Chancellor of England, and the most brutal. Although there is no written evidence, it is said that he sometimes held a magistrate's court at the Old Cock; pubs were often used as court rooms and the long narrow room upstairs was ideal.

Many visitors remark on a strange feeling when they enter the Old Cock. Ozolo Tawfik, the manager, comments that there are knocking noises where there are no pipes and that lights repeatedly flicker. The cleaner says:

I'm here a lot on my own and there's definitely something upstairs. I can hear bumps and bangs when the place is empty. I can cope with that, anything else and I'd be out through the door.

Nellie Copson, the Droitwich historian, can remember one incident:

Some time ago a young fellow asked if I would give a talk on Droitwich, and they had changed their meeting place from the Cock Inn to somewhere else, as the Cock Inn was a bit spooky. About three times he had heard a hard knocking on the door, he had got up to answer it but no-one was there'.

VILLAGERS MANAGED TO RESCUE THREE WINDOWS WHICH WERE INCORPORATED INTO THE REBUILDING OF THE OLD COCK INN.

DROITWICH

Trotter Hall

EVEN THE PEACH WALLS AND the piggy emblems fail to disguise the impressive grandeur of Trotter Hall. It was probably built in 1806 as a coaching inn. Known as the 'Copcut Elm Inn', it belonged to the wealthy landowner, John Amphlett, who installed Joseph Caswell as the first victualler. By 1916, it had been sold to Lewis Clarke and Company of Worcester, brewers and wine and spirit merchants, with a Welshman, Thomas Kench, as licensee. The locals remember it only as 'The Copcut Hotel' which was taken over in 1992 by the MAD O'Rourke chain to become Trotter Hall.

John Edwards was licensee in 1996 and he announced to the Worcester Evening News that he was thinking of leaving because of 'ghostly shadows, bumps and rumblings in the night and problems with the power supply'.

Later that year one of the regulars arrived and sat in a quiet corner of the bar. He ordered a Desperate Dan pie which was put in front of him. Suddenly he went white, sat bolt upright, picked up a chair and, guarding himself with it, ran through the whole pub then tried to get out of the fire exit door in the Shannon room. When this failed, he tried to smash a window. He had seen something in that pub which was so horrifying that they had to call an ambulance to calm him down. Sarah, the assistant manageress, says, 'He used to come once a week but he has never been back since'. She adds:

All kinds of strange things happen here. One evening recently there was a knocking on the fire exit door. I went to the door but nobody was there. As soon as I opened it the security light came on and it hadn't come on beforehand so nobody could have been there.

Caroline and John were clearing the tables in the bar one evening when Caroline discovered that she just could not physically go down one end of the bar. There was a solid invisible wall stopping her. She tried two or three times.

The telephone often stops working and the engineer can't find anything wrong with it. The day after the engineer had been, the telephone kept giving little rings but when you picked it up, nobody was there. On one occasion I dialled 1471 and the automated reply came that the last call had been the day before, even though I had just heard it ring.

We have a lot of problems with our power. The main power goes off quite regularly and when it does, the emergency lights sometimes don't work. One day the electrician was actually telling me that everything was OK when it all went off including the emergency lights. I was able to say, I told you! We have had new ones put in but they still don't work half the time. One morning last year, half-an-hour after the electricity had been checked, I went into the bar and smelt this awful sweet, sickly smell. Then as I switched the electricity off at the socket, there was a bang and a flash and the glass washer blew up. There was water everywhere. The smell had been the plastic container melting at the back of the glasswasher.

Sometimes these things are quite amusing. One of our staff was sitting on the loo one day and the hand dryer started off of its own accord. She shot out of the loo.

The door between the kitchen and the bar contains a small glass panel. Several of the staff and some guests have complained about a ghostly white face peering at them through the glass. Leon arrived as bartender in 1996 and had only been here a few weeks when:

Nobody had warned me about the ghost. At about 3.30 one afternoon, I was here on my own, doing a spring clean in the kitchen. I came out of the kitchen and went into the bar and I heard noises in the kitchen, as if someone was moving the equipment round. I thought, 'That's strange, there couldn't possibly be anyone in there'. Then the door from the kitchen swung right open as if someone had come through and when it went back again I saw a face in the window looking towards me. It was that of a middle-aged lady with a pale face and a blank expressionless look. I was shocked. I looked away then back again and nothing was there. I felt cold. I thought to myself, 'I don't believe it' and 'What the hell is going on?'. When I told people what I had seen everybody said, 'Oh, that must have been the ghost'.

Michelle has been head cook ever since Trotter Hall opened in 1992.

This is not a very bright pub, only half-lit, everything creaks and it's very spooky. Nearly every morning and especially on Sunday mornings when I'm on my own, this swing door opens and closes in a strange way. It opens, as if someone has pushed it open, stays there a second as if someone is walking through, then closes. When it closes it doesn't swing, it's just as if someone carefully replaces it to its original position. At first I didn't think much about the swing door and assumed it was something to do with the extractor fan, but when I tried to recreate it, I couldn't. Then I thought it might be one of the children playing a joke so I rushed to the door several times to catch them but no-one was there. Local people say that there is a ghost here by the name of White who was hung in one of the rooms upstairs in the days when it was a coaching inn. Now we just call out, 'Good morning, Mr White!'.

We were talking about this one day and we were all laughing when suddenly, the door shot open and hit a table with such force that everything was shaking. It was really weird. We all screamed, ran into the Shannon room and nervously lit up, then we sat there, puffing furiously. We always considered the Shannon room to be safe, as this and an extension to the kitchen was built in 1992, and the ghost always seemed to appear in the old part which dates back to the beginning of the nineteenth century.

However, I discovered one morning that the Shannon room wasn't always safe. The landlady said to me, 'Would you do me a favour, go and get me a packet of cigarettes from the machine in the Shannon room?' In those days a packet was £3, so I put this into the machine but only £2 registered. The missing £1 wasn't even in the returned coins. I had to go and ask her for another £1. About three-quarters of an hour later we were all sitting in the Shannon room and all of a sudden the £1 coin shot out of the machine, flew across the room to where I was sitting, hit me on the arm then dropped on the floor. It could not fly across the room from the returned coins compartment because there was a lip at the bottom. I looked at it and I said, 'Well I never, there's the missing coin' then we all yelled because we knew we were not safe even in the Shannon room any more.

I once felt as if someone was standing in the bar. There was this cold area, tall and about fifteen inches across. I stepped into it and walked out of it again. I said to Doreen, 'You walk just here' and she could feel it as well. It was so scary that we ran into the Shannon room and had to sit and have a smoke. In the summer of 1994 nearly all the kitchen staff were sitting round a table in the Shannon room, I had my back to the centre of the room and Doreen was sitting opposite. Suddenly I saw her eyes follow something. She said, 'Somebody just walked out from behind the bar. I got up and went to have a look but nobody was there. She's not the only person to have seen an apparition. Christine, who was the assistant manager in about 1993, had almost finished locking up when she saw a man walking across the room. She said later that he was small and dumpy with a peaked cap pulled down over his head. She said, 'Excuse me, can I help you?' but he disappeared through the wall.

I looked after the pub for a week while the manager and his wife were on holiday. Every night something happened to me. My husband and my son came over and we slept upstairs, then my husband left at 6 am to go to work. I had a big bunch of keys and at night I would go round and lock up. The manager left us a long list of instructions and my husband would follow me with the instructions in his hand reading them out as I locked all the doors so he was able to double check. We would laugh to ourselves at all these precise instructions. One morning, when I came down, two of the doors were wide open. If someone had come in he would have activated the alarms.

Another morning I came down, and as I walked into the kitchen all the cooker fires went pow! and they all ignited of their own accord. They couldn't have been left on overnight as it was really cold in there. You have never seen me move so fast out of the kitchen!

A little old lady came into the pub when it was being enlarged and said, 'If he doesn't like it, he'll let you know'. We don't know who she was referring to but some of the old customers have suggested that the ghost could be that of the old gardener. The new extensions have been built over the garden. Evidently, he didn't like it because on the open day we had 250 people packed in here, all eating, and the power went off, flickered and then it came back on again then went off for an hour. The electrician couldn't find anything wrong.

Mr White, or the gardener, comes and goes with managers. The first three managers had problems with the ghost - in fact the first couple saw it - but since the present manager, Paul, came, the ghost seems to have quietened down a bit..

☎ **01905 778845**

→ Trotter Hall stands isolated on the A38 to Worcester, just outside Droitwich

⌚ Mon–Fri: 1130–1500
1730–2300
Sat–Sun: 1200–all day

🍴 Home-cooked meals and bar snacks (including Balti) plus carvery on a Sunday

🎴 Yes

🍺 Real ales, also their own ales

ⓘ A function room takes 250 standing or 180 sitting. They have all kinds of bands, with Folk and Irish music on Tuesday, Friday, Saturday and Sunday, and occasional Thursdays. This pub is one of the MAD O'Rourke chain. They have a pub trail where you get a reward if you visit other pubs in the trail. Trotter Hall is the place to visit if you need cheering up. It's great for a fun night out, any age group.

DROITWICH · COPCUTT

Station Hotel

☎ **01384 253418**

Non-residents:
Mon–Fri: 1730–2300
Sat–Sun: 1900–2300

→ Opposite the entrance to
Dudley Zoo and Castle

🍴 Home-cooked bar and
restaurant meals

ⓘ 38 rooms, both single
and double. Also four
rooms for hire

DUDLEY RAILWAY STATION was opened in 1850 but for half a century after this the town had no appropriate inn for rail travellers. A licence was granted in 1896 for the Dudley and Wolverhampton breweries to develop a hotel, which was unimaginatively christened 'The Station Hotel'.

Jamie, of the Dudley Ghost Tours, has more than one macabre story about the building:

I have heard from many people that the Station Hotel is haunted. It is supposed to have two ghosts. The first is that of Mr Parry, better known as the Tipton Slasher, a national boxing champion. He came out of retirement in order to fight a smaller boxer. It so happened that living in Dudley at that time was a man with amazing psychic powers, generally known as the Dudley Devil. He said to Mr Parry, 'Don't box him, you will lose and you will be humiliated'. However, Mr Parry took no notice of this, went ahead with the fight and subsequently lost. The trials and tribulations of his defeat were so humiliating that he hung himself in the cellar. His ghost is said to wander around down there.

There is also said to be the ghost of a servant girl murdered by her evil master. He hid her body in a vat of oil.

I worked behind the bar for a couple of years and one morning in 1995, one of the residents came down as white as a sheet. I knew him quite well, as he and his wife stayed here quite a lot. He said, 'You won't believe the night I had last night'. I said, 'Try me'. Evidently, they were in the habit of going to sleep with the telly switched on but with the sound turned right down. He woke up in the night to see that the telly had been switched off. He switched it on again and by the dim, flickering light of the television he saw the figure of a man in a black pointed hat standing by the curtains. He lay there for some time watching it, terrified out of his wits, until it faded away. His girlfriend was asleep and so she didn't see it but she had strange nightmares about there being something in the room.

For a hair-raising hour or so listening to more of Jamie's ghost stories, telephone Dudley Zoo and Castle on **01384 215300** and ask to join one of his evening ghost tours.

BY THE DIM, FLICKERING LIGHT
OF THE TELEVISION HE SAW
THE FIGURE OF A MAN

DUDLEY

Old White Swan ⓘ

no longer in existence

THE OLD WHITE SWAN IS NO LONGER IN EXISTENCE BUT IT STOOD AT NUMBER THREE, CASTLE STREET, AND WAS ALSO KNOWN AS 'The Wooden House', the 'Coconut Grove' and the 'Rock Garden'. The first licensee on record was William Pinnock in 1822, followed by James Wilkinson, in 1835, a vice and anvil manufacturer who had fallen on hard times.

The Swan Inn had the reputation of being haunted. It was built on the foundations of a nunnery and spectral nuns were said to walk out from the walls. The grave of Edmund Croaker, the eighteenth century executioner is buried in a graveyard nearby and he, too, was said to appear from time to time. In addition, the Swan once saw a savage murder committed within its walls.

DURING THE 1860'S THE LICENSEE WAS WILLIAM WILKINSON, PERHAPS THE SON OF JAMES, WHO MADE ANVILS AND VICES ON THE PREMISES. HE HAD WORKSHOPS OUT THE BACK BUT HIS MOST VALUABLE TOOLS WERE STORED IN THE CELLAR. HE WAS FRIENDLY WITH THE LOCAL BAILIFF, WILLIAM ROWLANDS, A HARD MAN. ROWLANDS SPENT MUCH OF HIS SPARE TIME AT THE SWAN AND OFTEN USED THE CELLAR. WHEN HE WAS WORKING DOWN THERE ONE NIGHT, CRIES OF TERROR WERE HEARD BY THE NEIGHBOURS. THE NEXT MORNING, THE BAILIFF DID NOT EMERGE SO THE PARISH CONSTABLE BROKE DOWN THE DOOR AND DISCOVERED THAT ROWLAND'S HEAD HAD BEEN CRUSHED BETWEEN THE JAWS OF A LARGE VICE.

ONE STRANGE FACT IN THE CASE WAS THAT ALL THE DOORS HAD BEEN BOLTED FROM THE INSIDE. IT WOULD HAVE BEEN IMPOSSIBLE FOR A MURDERER TO GET AWAY. THE MURDERER WAS NEVER FOUND AND INDEED, MANY OF THE LOCALS WONDERED IF WILLIAM ROWLANDS HAD RECEIVED RETRIBUTION FOR HIS RUTHLESS INHUMANITY NOT IN THIS WORLD BUT THE NEXT.

Shrewsbury Arms

→ 2 Wolverhampton Street, off the High Street

THE SHREWSBURY ARMS WAS IN EXISTENCE BY 1819 when it was known as the Talbot Hotel. To quote John Richards in his Pubs and Breweries of the Old Dudley Borough, 'Known locally as The Cow Shed it had a lot of character—too much for Wolverhampton & Dudley Breweries Ltd, it was dragged up-market, gutted, and is now the Shrewsbury Arms'.

Marlene, who is now licensee of the Rock Tavern in Caunsall, used to do relief work and round about 1981 she was at the Shrewsbury Arms for three weeks.

ONE MORNING AFTER I HAD BEEN THERE FOR ABOUT A WEEK, I WAS IN THE BAR ON MY OWN. THE CLEANER HAD LEFT AND MY HUSBAND HAD GONE TO WORK. I WENT DOWN THE CELLAR TO CHECK THE BEERS—I USED TO DO THIS BEFORE I POPPED OUT TO GET MY SHOPPING. THE CELLARS WENT A LONG WAY UNDERGROUND, THE BEER WAS STORED IN THE MAIN CELLAR BUT THERE WERE OTHER CELLARS GOING OFF WHICH WERE UNUSED. I HAPPENED TO LOOK UP AND IN ONE OF THE DISUSED CELLARS I SAW THIS APPARITION LOOKING AT ME. HE WAS A LITTLE OLD MAN AND HE HAD A CAP ON. THE NEXT DAY I SAID TO THE LADY WHO WAS HELPING, 'PLEASE DON'T GO HOME UNTIL I HAVE BEEN DOWN THE CELLAR'.

I SAW HIM AGAIN ON THE FRIDAY AFTERNOON OF THE FOLLOWING WEEK, WHEN I WAS SORTING OUT THE SMALL CHANGE READY FOR THE BANK. THE BAR WAS A SQUARISH ROOM AND IN THE MIDDLE WAS A PILLAR WITH A LITTLE SHELF ROUND IT WHERE PEOPLE USED TO PUT THEIR DRINKS. I SENSED SOMETHING STRANGE AND THEN I SAW THIS LITTLE OLD MAN RUN BEHIND THE PILLAR. I SAID TO HIM, 'PLEASE, I AINT SCARED OF YOU BUT DON'T COME TO SEE ME WHEN I'M ON MY OWN, IT FRIGHTENS ME THEN'.

I ONLY SAW HIM THIS TWICE BUT I USED TO SENSE THAT HE WAS THERE AND I USED TO TALK TO HIM WHEN TIMES WERE DIFFICULT. I CALLED HIM OLD JOE.

THE
MALT
SHOVEL

FOOD
FRESHLY
COOKED
PUB MEALS

DUDLEY

Malt Shovel Inn

JAMIE, OF THE DUDLEY GHOST TOURS (01384 215300) MAINTAINS THAT TOWER STREET IS THE MOST HAUNTED STREET IN DUDLEY, AND THE MALT SHOVEL IS AT NUMBER 46.

An unpretentious Georgian building, it is one of the oldest public houses in Dudley and was made a listed building as long ago as 1947. Prior to 1860 it was known as the Lord Wellington and was important enough for the landlord to issue his own coins, known as tokens.

The Malt Shovel hit the headlines on 7 March 1926, when the licensee's son, fourteen year old Jimmy Bayliss, was found hacked to death in bed. His twenty-four year old half brother, Joseph Flavell, a crane driver, confessed to murdering him with an axe and was sentenced to death. A week later the death sentence was commuted to penal servitude.

A blue, shifting form, known as 'the blue boy' has been seen more than once in one of the upper rooms. In addition, says Jamie, an apparition the size of a small adult has appeared in the Lounge Bar area, along with a ghostly black dog.

 01384 252735

 Tower Street begins across the road from the zoo entrance

 Mon: morning only
Tue–Sat: 1100–2300
Sun: closed

 Yes

Bar snacks

 Yes

A Banks's pub

DUDLEY

Vauxhall Beefeater

THE VALE OF EVESHAM IS FAMOUS FOR ITS FRUIT AND

Mrs Walker, who lives in Wales, has a son who usually spends a few weeks each autumn fruit-picking in the Evesham area. He wanted his mother to see the fruit trees in blossom and so, on the first Saturday in April 1997, they were driven over by two friends.

There were four of us; me and my son, and my son's friend and his mother. We called at Evesham town and decided to stop for a drink at the Vauxhall. We sat at a table on the left which has a little window behind and another at the side.

I was sitting there, drinking my pineapple juice and talking to the others, when I felt something tap my shoulder. I turned round to see a man in his late forties, obviously well-educated, with a tall black hat, a white blouse or shirt with long sleeves hanging down and lace around the cuffs, and a black waistcoat with two rows of buttons. I could only see him down to the waist as he was standing behind the settee, in spite of the fact that there was not enough room between the settee and the wall for anyone to stand. He was hanging there in mid-air. I went cold all over and the hairs on my arms rose. I felt that my mind was linking into his or vice versa and I knew that he had been a doctor and that I was sitting in his house.

As I looked at him he raised an arm and pointed at a small window on the other side of the room. I felt that he was anxious that I should look out of the window. I could see the wall of a building opposite, the street was cobbled and I saw that there were huge fires burning down each side of the street. I had this feeling that something terrible had happened. Then he disappeared. I was the only one who had seen him.

I asked the landlady if she knew anything about the history of the Vauxhall and the area but she said that she had not been there for long and she didn't know it.

I have had these experiences before when I seem to sense something which has happened in the past. I usually go to see my local librarian, tell him what I have seen and he tries to put it into some kind of context. I'm not very good at drawing but I did a rough sketch of the man that I had seen. He looked in his reference books and he said that he thought that I had visited Evesham in the time of the great plague. He didn't know what the fires were but I remember reading somewhere that in some areas there were so many plague victims that they were piled up in the streets then the bodies were burned in the streets and the ashes scattered on consecrated ground. I wondered if this had anything to do with it.

I can't say that I enjoyed my visit to Evesham. I didn't know anything about the town before I went but I felt that it had so much history and so many things have happened there that I found the place quite weird.

What the librarian in Wales did not know was that the building seen by Mrs Walker opposite the Vauxhall, was the Almonry, which has now been converted into a museum. As long ago as 714 Bishop Egwin founded a great abbey at Evesham which, despite rebuilding and additions in later centuries, has now almost completely disappeared. The Almonry was the home of the Almoner whose duty it was to distribute the alms to the poor and needy. Consequently, it could be possible that a physician or someone in that line of business lived opposite the Almonry. Plague victims could have been brought to this physician and also to the nearby Abbey gate.

Another theory comes from Tony Whiting, Manager of the Information Centre based in the Almonry, who also knows a bit about the history of the Vauxhall:

The area on which the Vauxhall is built was once part of the abbey farmyard. Where Abbey Road now runs the Barton Gate would have been situated. The first reference to the Vauxhall was in 1859. The inn was known as a 'tiddleywink' or common ale house. In 1928 it was rebuilt when Abbey Road was constructed.

My only thought was that the man described by Mrs Walker appears to have been dressed in a costume more reminiscent of the 17th century. In 1644 Charles I stayed in Evesham and the town was stormed in May 1645. This may have led to fires in the streets but this is by no means conclusive.

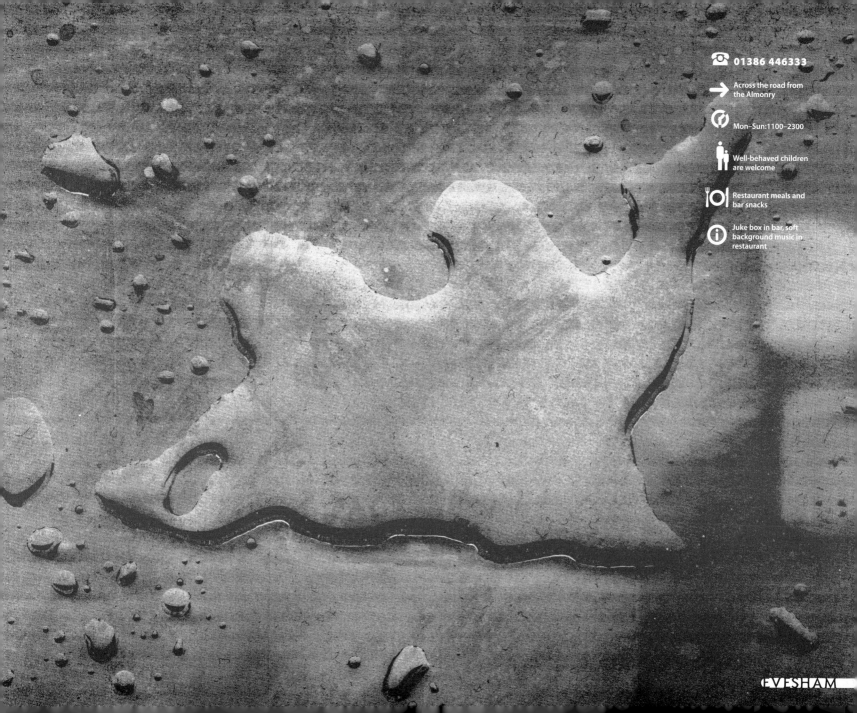

☎ **01386 446333**

➡ Across the road from
the Almonry

⟳ Mon–Sun:1100–2300

♟ Well-behaved children
are welcome

🍴 Restaurant meals and
bar snacks

ⓘ Juke box in bar, soft
background music in
restaurant

EVESHAM

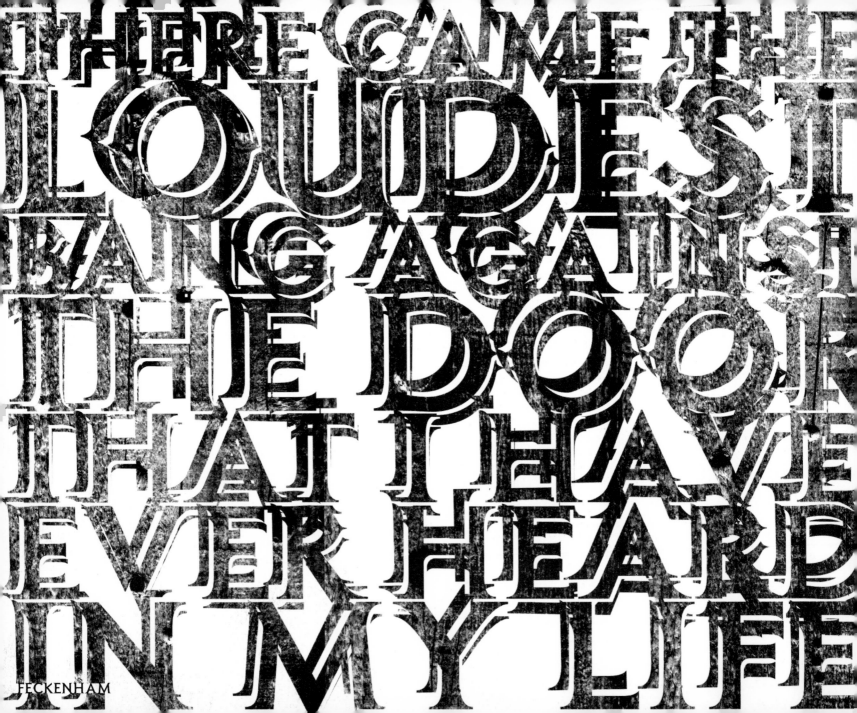

THERE CAME THE
LOUDEST
BANG AGAINST
THE DOOR
THAT I HAVE
EVER HEARD
IN MY LIFE

FECKENHAM

Rose & Crown

IN MEDIEVAL TIMES ALEHOUSES PLAYED AN IMPORTANT PART IN CHURCH LIFE AND SOME CHURCHES EVEN HAD THEIR OWN ALEHOUSE.

The Rose and Crown is so near to Feckenham Parish Church that it must surely have been associated with it. And as the Church is Norman, the original Rose and Crown could possibly date back to early medieval times. Its name suggests that it is at least 400 years old as many alehouses were renamed the Rose and Crown in about 1485 to celebrate the end of the Wars of the Roses. By 1843, when the licensee was James James, it was known as the Old Rose and Crown. It was in two distinct parts, one of which belonged to James and the other to the Lord of the Manor.

Ed Doolan, the well-known radio presenter, particularly remembers a visit there.

We had an incident at the Rose and Crown in Feckenham several years ago when I had just joined the station. Beside the pub was a long building which had store rooms downstairs and offices upstairs. The door to the store rooms was locked and sealed. We were told that a ghost was there which was continuing day and night. They had a lot of strange things happening, this ghost used to muck about with the office equipment during the day and they used to have to say to it, 'Now come on, clear off!'.

It was in the evening, towards winter, and it was dark. We had Ethel Lakins with us, the clairvoyant, and one of my colleagues, Stuart Roper, who has since passed on. While we were chatting to people and recording, he was teasing. He was saying ,'Come on ghostie, where are you? we want you ghostie'. Suddenly, from the other side of that door there came the loudest bang against the door that I have ever heard in my life. The whole door shook. I would have sworn that somebody on the other side had kicked it but nobody was there. Stuart took off to the other side of the car park faster than any human being has ever run.

It was a remarkable programme. I shall never forget that one.

In 1983 Mr and Mrs McWalter arrived with their four (later five) children. Perhaps the entity decided to seek a more peaceful environment because it has not since manifested itself.

 01527 89218

 Opposite Feckenham Church; Feckenham is about six miles south of Bromsgrove on the B4090

 Mon–Sun: 1100–1500 1800–2300

 Yes

 Home-cooked restaurant food and bar snacks

 Yes

 Special beers supplied by Banks's brewery

(i) Owned and managed by the McWalter family since 1983. The pub has a reputation for good, reasonably-priced food. Occasionally live Cajan music. In *Pub Walks in Worcestershire*

☎ **01527 821790**

On the B4091, between Hanbury and Bromsgrove

Mon–Sat: 1130–1430
1730–2300
Sun: 1200–1500
1900–2230

Over 14 years in bar area for meals. Under 14 in conservatory for meals.

Home-cooked restaurant meals and bar snacks

Conservatory and large beer garden

Owned by Whitbread, it offers a selection of cask ales and is renowned for its good clean beers

ⓘ Live music is provided during the Beer Festival in July. In the *Good Food Pub Guide*, and mentioned in *Pub Walks in Worcestershire*

Country Girl

DURING THE EARLY 1980'S, THE LICENSEE CLAIMED THIS WAS THE MOST HAUNTED INN IN THE COUNTRY. THE BAR WAS OFTEN PACKED WITH PEOPLE HOPING FOR A GLIMPSE OF THE GHOST.

Until about 1982, the Country Girl Inn was the easternmost cottage in a row of five agricultural workers' cottages. The next cottage was tenanted, the next two were derelict and the last (the largest) was let. The bar area was only as wide as a man's outstretched arms and a tiny restaurant seated 14. Accommodation was available upstairs. For a few years before 1965, the licensee was a retired school-teacher, but when his son was eighteen, the licence was handed over to the son. Thus Mark Hardman became one of the youngest licensees on record.

The locals say that although he was a kind and considerate man,' he was as near as you will ever get to Basil Fawlty'. The regulars never quite knew what Mark would do next. There was the occasion that he returned from Birmingham Wholesale market with two kilograms of alligators, and alligator meat was on the menu for a few nights. A local remembers 'It was very tough, even my spaniel spat it out and he will eat anything'. Then there was the instance when a regular arrived in his Rolls Royce, and, quite by chance, a visitor arrived, also in a Rolls Royce.

These two cars were the only ones in the car park and then a female arrived in her little Minor 1000 and parked alongside, Mark said to her, 'It's Rolls Royce's only tonight' and wouldn't let the poor lady in!

Staff needed a sense of humour when working with Mark which was not always appreciated by the clientele. There was one memorable moment when a customer asked what was in the omelette. 'Anything Mark can scrape off the kitchen floor', said the barmaid. She did not know that she was speaking to the local Health Inspector.

It was while Mark was the licensee that the Country Girl was said to be haunted. During the 1980's the inn was packed with people hoping for a paranormal experience. Mark told the press that ghostly footsteps climbed the stairs each night and walked towards his bedroom. Sue Jinks, the cook, was getting lunch ready when she heard a creaking noise and four plates shot out of the wall cabinet without breaking. Liz Chandler was tidying outside tables when the inn sign, weighing a ton, fell for no apparent reason and narrowly missed her.

The Hanbury area is well-known for the ghost of Emma Vernon, who lived at Hanbury Hall at the end of the eighteenth century. Despite being married to a member of the aristocratic Cecil family, she ran away with the local curate. She was buried, at her own request, in unconsecrated ground at Hanbury church.

There was a small pool outside the rear of the Country Girl in the 1970's, which features in the next anecdote:

I was sitting in the car park, waiting for my girl-friend to finish working in the kitchen, when I saw this shape rise up out of the pond. It was a human-shaped cloud of white fog, a female figure, and it just stayed in the one place, it didn't move about.

He ran into the kitchen in a distressed state and had to sit down for twenty minutes before he could drive home.

In 1982, the Brewery converted the whole of the site. The three adjacent cottages became an extension of the inn and the cottage at the western end became the manager's house. A conglomeration of sheds and run-down out houses at the rear was made into a car park. Mark ceased to be a tenant shortly before the redevelopment started and moved away, apparently taking Emma Vernon with him, as she has not been seen since.

HANBURY

01684 592686

 Near Upton-on-Severn, on the Upton/Malvern road. Take the third turn left off the B4211

 Mon–Sat: 1100–14/1500
1900–2300
Sun: close 2230

 Allowed but not encouraged

 Grills and other main courses, starters and sweets as bar snacks

 Front patio

 A thousand different beers have been offered since records began six years ago. Two regular and three others on at any time, all from small independent breweries

(i) One room is available for accommodation. Live music is performed on Sunday evenings, usually a guitar and vocal. Awards: CAMRA National Pub of the Year 1993 and CAMRA West Midlands Pub of the Year in 1997. Featured in *Pub Walks in Worcestershire*.

Three Kings

THIS IS AN ELEGANT AND HISTORIC BUILDING IN A PICTURESQUE SETTING, near to the church. During the cold weather real fires burn in the inglenook fireplaces. Behind the pub's Georgian front are ancient beams which were once ship's timbers and date back to the sixteenth or even the fifteenth century. The Three Kings was built on the site of a medieval church house and continued to have close links with the church through the centuries. Various parish events were held there and a room upstairs, approached by an outside staircase, was used for tithe audits and club meetings. The Lounge was once the house next door, which was assimilated into the pub probably during the 1960's. As the house had been occupied by 'Old Nell', the Lounge is now known as 'Nell's Room'.

The Three Kings has been held by the Robert's family since 1911. Mrs Roberts Senior commented, 'I don't think we want a ghost', however, one was seen there on 8th July 1981. The lady concerned was so impressed that she went home and wrote down a description of the apparition so that she would not forget any details.

I saw the ghost standing to the left of the fireplace, holding something like knitting in her right hand. It was a short, plump woman, quite elderly, with dark eyes and pink cheeks, and she was smiling. She had either white hair or a white cap, lace or snood, under a tall, Welsh-type hat with a flat top—the hat was made of leather (it looked like a Pontefract cake). She had a white shawl round her shoulders over a red bodice and skirt. She was wearing a black overskirt looped up at the sides and she had rather long shoes, cut off square at the toes. She was quite solid, you couldn't see through her at all. The only way I knew it was a ghost was because the back of her skirt went through the wall and parts of her were missing.

While I was standing there I went to the bar and asked the landlord if the pub was haunted. he dismissed the idea in an abrupt, matter-of-fact way. She was there for a few minutes, then the next time I looked, she had gone.

A local man, Ray, was friendly with the son and daughter of Mrs Roberts Junior, and comments:

This sounds just like a description of Old Nell. I knew her well, we often went into her house and she was dressed just like this. I never saw her in a large black hat but people used to say that she wore one whenever she went into the village. She passed away about twenty years ago. I was very sorry as she was a likeable person.

HANLEY CASTLE

White Swan

THE WHITE SWAN IS AN OLD COACHING INN, WHERE STAGE COACHES PULLED IN on the long journey from Birmingham to London. At first sight it appears to be Tudor but, in actual fact, this is one of the oldest buildings in Henley, dating back to 1358. The building was modernised in the seventeenth century by having a false front fitted.

When Jacky Bollard became manager in 1985, she was warned about the grey lady. However, the following incident is the only one to occur during her time as manager.

In the late spring of 1989 we had a party of six adults. Two of them, husband and wife, stayed in room seventeen. During the night—

they were woken up by a violent tugging at the quilt

It was rather a sitcom situation, with the wife thinking it was the husband and the husband thinking it was the wife, and it was some minutes before they woke up sufficiently to realise that neither of them was pulling the quilt and it was jerking of its own accord. Alarmed, they sat up in bed and saw, moving about the room, dark, misty shadows of half-a-dozen people which faded away after a few seconds.

The husband took this more calmly than the wife and eventually dropped off to sleep but the wife remained awake. It was then that she saw the grey lady. She described it later as the pale face of a young woman staring out from quite a bulky body which was just a mass of dark grey. She thought the ghost might have looked shapeless because she was wearing a cloak. The grey lady soon faded away.

The locals say that this is the apparition of a maid who once worked here and lived on the top floor. She was having an affair with one of the local gentry and the two used to meet in her room. One night they had a disagreement; rumour has it that he was trying to end the relationship. Things became very heated and she was pushed down the stairs, dying from her injuries.

 01564 792623

 Number 100, High Street

Bar meals are available each day of the week. Bar has open fires

 Three hand-pulled bitters, lagers, bottled beers and a full range of spirits and liqueurs

 All rooms en suite and one with four poster bed.

HENLEY-IN-ARDEN

Bull's Head

THERE MUST ONCE HAVE BEEN A WELL-KNOWN BULL AT INKBERROW because both pubs in the village are named after a bull. The Old Bull is on the village green and has been featured in *The Archers* radio programme. The Bull's Head, which stands on the main road through Inkberrow, is equally popular, chiefly because of its reputation for good food. It is thought to date back to the sixteenth century.

Garry, the present manager, moved to Inkberrow in 1990 and felt so at home in the village and so comfortable in the Bull's Head that he bought it in 1993. While he was redecorating he uncovered a small secret room off a bedroom in the old part of the building, probably a priest's hiding hole. He has left it as it was, except that a piece of glass has been inserted in the bedroom wall. It is therefore possible to book sixteenth century accommodation here with en suite facilities and a priest's hiding hole.

The Bulls Head has the reputation of being haunted but, as with many other old pubs, the ghost comes or goes according to the licensee. Garry has only experienced one curious incident, when water appeared to drip from a beam in the bar but there were no pipes nearby and no puddle or damp patch appeared on the floor.

However, when the previous licensee, Debbie Ison, arrived at the pub in the 1960's, she and her husband didn't believe in ghosts but by the time she left in 1993 she was convinced that the place was haunted. She, too, had problems with phantom water from the same beam:

One Sunday morning, I was in the bar serving breakfast to a guest on holiday from Yorkshire when:

Suddenly, a steady trickle of liquid came down from the ceiling. It was just as if someone was pouring half-a-pint of beer from the beam. The guest said, 'You've got a leak'. 'That's strange', I said, 'There's no water above there!' and there isn't, just an empty room. I looked to see how large the pool was—and couldn't find it!'. 'Where the hell is the puddle?' asked the York-shireman. It was quite funny, we looked everywhere, even down our boots, but we never found it.

This was not the only strange occurrence.

When Gordon Quiney was here, he often helped out behind the bar and to save him going home late at night he used to stay the night in one of our single rooms. Each morning he got up very early to let the cleaner in. One morning, when I came down, he said 'Where did you get to? He said that he heard me calling him at about six o'clock, so he got up and went to the door, but no-one was there. A few minutes later this happened again.

My parents came to stay with us during the January of the following year, as it was my mother's birthday. After the pub had closed, we locked the doors and all the family sat in the lounge, except for my father who went off to bed. Suddenly, my husband heard my father calling him. He went upstairs but my father was fast asleep. Mystified, he came downstairs and this time we all heard a man's voice calling my husband's name. My mother was so frightened she went behind the bar and wouldn't come out.

A few days later something happened that I first put down to the fact that I was very tired after the Christmas and New Year rush. As I was coming down the staircase, I saw the door at the bottom open and caught a glimpse of a train of a pale-coloured frilly dress—just as if someone had opened the door and pulled the train through. It was so real I jumped down the stairs in a couple of seconds and shouted 'Gotcha!' but no-one was there.

Two of our guests have seen an apparition here. One came down in the morning and said, 'I didn't believe you when you said my room was haunted but I woke up and saw this woman sitting on my bed. Then she vanished'. He described her as having a long pale-coloured dress. In February 1991 we had a guest staying here and he came down in the morning saying, 'Is my room haunted?'.

He said that he got out of bed early in the morning and went to the bathroom but just happened to look over his shoulder and saw someone else getting out of his bed.

Another landlady before Debbie, Betty Kacorevic, was at the Bull's Head for nine years and she had an unusual experience:

We had an American staying here on the first floor and early one morning I heard him cry out. I was sleeping on the top floor, I leaped out of bed and went to the top of

the stairs. There she was, the ghost, walking up the staircase towards me. She had entered the American's room then continued up to the top storey.

She was absolutely beautiful, just perfect. She was about fortyish and she had long blonde hair and a white silky dress and she sort of fluttered up the stairs. I was frightened when I heard the American shout but when I saw her I was not afraid at all. She never spoke. She got to the top then just disappeared.

The American wouldn't have it that she was a ghost. He kept asking where the beautiful blonde was. I kept saying, 'There is no blonde'.

It is not only the landladies who have stories to tell. Sarah is now a housewife living in the Beoley area.

When I was in my early teens I was very friendly with the daughter of the licensee, Claire, and I often went there and stayed overnight. I usually slept in Claire's room which was on the top floor and on the extreme right if you are facing the building. One night, in the summer of 1977, I was awoken from my sleep by something cold and wet touching my side, from my shoulder down to my hips. I assumed that I had turned over in my sleep, taking the bedclothes with me and leaving my side exposed. I quickly sat

upright in bed and was just in time to hear a 'whoosh' as something shot from my side across the room and out through the closed door. There was nothing to be seen, I could only hear the noise. I had been most careful to close the door and lock it from the inside before I went to bed.

In March 1990, Pam Pearce was helping out, doing the ironing, when:

I felt as if someone was there. I have often had this feeling before and put it down to the fact that we treat the ghost as a joke and creep up on each other. However, this time I turned round and saw a young girl just fading. She was wearing a long, pale blue print dress with a train, and she had on her head a hat with a scarf over it. I would think her clothes dated back to the sixteenth or seventeenth century. She had long fair hair and was very young and pretty, about 18 or 20, I would guess, but it was all over so soon. I said 'Hullo' but she quickly faded away.

According to local tradition, a young seamstress died here in about the seventeenth century and it looks as if she comes back to her place of work from time to time. The day I saw her, the landlady had left her sewing things out and I think this was what prompted our ghost to make a return visit.

 01386 792233

 On main road through Inkberrow (A422)

 Mon–Sun: 1100–1500 1700–2300

 Yes

 Restaurant meals

 Outdoor eating area

 Own brew known as 'Bull's Head Bitter'.

ⓘ Reputation for good, reasonably-priced food, all of which is cooked by the owner/manager or under his supervision. Accommodation: Five double rooms.

INKBERROW

Ye Olde Severn Stars

GENUINE OLDE WORLDE PUBS ARE BECOMING INCREASING-LY DIFFICULT TO FIND, but Ye Olde Severn Stars is one of them. This is the oldest pub in central Kidderminster, the plot of land on which it stands was mentioned in the Domesday book. No-one knows when two cottages were built on this land, but they were converted into a pub in about 1792. As a Grade II listed building, the licensee is unable to make any alterations with the result that the most recent furnishings are Victorian. It has two small rooms known as the Full Bar and the Back Bar. During the cold weather, a fire is lit in the tiny grate of the Full Bar.

According to the locals, they heard from their parents and grandparents that Ye Olde Severn Stars has always

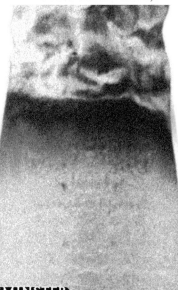

been a place of ill-repute. For many years it served as the local brothel, or 'pick-up joint'. In addition, its location near the river Stour made it ideal for smuggling. This is borne out by the fact that the cellars have an adjoining room with two tunnels running from it, thought to be escape routes. One leads under the road to the Barrels public house, the other leads in another direction to the local fish and chip shop and beyond. As far as anyone knows they have not been fully explored as they are full of rubble and garbage and have been blocked off at some stage.

The pub was once a coaching inn although the stables at the back have long since disappeared. When armies used to pass through, officers would sleep in the bedrooms while the troops were billeted in the stables with the horses.

Its colourful history seems to have left behind a character or two. The grey lady has been known for many years. According to *Haunted Pubs* by Marc Alexander (published in 1984), Mrs Freda Holloway was in the bar when she heard her name called and turned to see a woman in a white dress of about the 1900 period standing at the end of the bar. The woman disappeared but Mrs Holloway saw her again several times after that. The landlady stated that several customers had heard their name called. The local press ran the story, after which a reader wrote to the

newspaper saying that her mother had been born on the premises at the turn of the century and she, too, had seen an apparition which was then wearing a large white apron.

Two years previously, Ted Sanchez had been the licensee. In December 1982, he told Mike Pryce of the *Worcester Evening News*:

We didn't know it was haunted before we came, but it wouldn't have made any difference anyway. I was a great disbeliever until now. The regulars told me strange things happened but I didn't take any notice. After all, you often get talk like that.

The first things that started to happen were that the gas taps in the cellar kept getting turned off. There's normally about two to three weeks supply in a gas cylinder and no-one would have any reason to go near them, but you'd be pulling the pints in the bar when suddenly everything would stop. I'd have to go down to the cellar and find that the taps were turned off—just like that, with no-one around.

The ghost is quite adept at learning people's names and often I have heard a soft woman's voice calling me, but when I go to answer there's no-one about. Another favourite trick is to move glasses on the bar top. You lay the glasses out, turn your back and they've shifted positions without anyone about.

We have a deep freeze in the living quarters with the control covered by a special guard. This appliance, in full view of the family, switched itself off. No-one had tampered with the guard, there was no change in the electrical current and no undue vibrations. Yet it went off. I had to remove the guard to turn it back on again. We couldn't believe it.

Then one night we were talking about this in the bar when one fellow said, 'I don't believe in God or The Devil' and with that a plate suddenly flew off the wall and landed on the floor! There is no way that plate could have slipped off, it was on a wide ledge with several others yet it suddenly shot away from the wall on to the carpet. It killed that conversation I tell you.

It nearly bounced off the head of one of the pub staff. He was a bit shaken up. But we don't think the ghost meant to hurt anyone. It's definitely not a bad ghost, It's a bit of a laugh really, more of a mischief than anything else. You get quite used to it.

We've kept a tab on the number of things that happen and they usually peak between the 10th to the 18th of each month and then quieten down again. It can be a nuisance more than anything else.

Some of the bar girls refuse to go down into the cellar because that's where they believe the Grey Lady lives.

Mark, who became the licensee in 1996, says:

It is definitely eerie and creepy here. All kinds of strange things happen. One evening after we had closed and the staff had gone home, I was cleaning up behind the bar when I noticed that someone had left a packet of cigarettes on the table. A few minutes later I thought I saw something moving on the table and the cigarettes were on the floor about five feet away.

Recently, in the space of one week, several things inexplicably fell of the wall. One of them was an old framed photo in the back bar, this had been hung quite securely with a ring and a nail (I don't see how I could make it more secure) and twice in the same week it fell on the floor. It hasn't done that before or since.

The taps for the beers are sometimes turned off. That's weird. Down the cellar there is a row of about a dozen little valves, one to each beer. Occasionally, instead of them all being open they're closed off. It happens overnight when there's nobody around—we notice it in the morning when the previous evening they have been running OK.

We have always had trouble with the telephone. Every day, something else is wrong with it. Sometimes it will work, sometimes it won't. Just

lately, the volume has been going really low for some unknown reason.

We have recently acquired a dog which usually spends the night in the Back Bar, but between twelve and one in the morning (the witching hour) he comes into the Full Bar and barks and barks and gets very agitated.

The regulars tell me that the culprit is a grey lady. Whatever it is, I have never felt threatened or frightened. At worst, this place is spooky. I don't mind the grey lady so long as she doesn't start drinking the stock!

The barman, Rob, knows all about the grey lady.

I have seen the grey lady twice but I experience her more through the tricks that she plays. She stops the barrels off downstairs (that has happened quite a lot of times) and she turns the lights off downstairs —I always leave them on. She does things like that.

It was one night in 1995, getting on for midnight, when I first saw her. Most of the lights had been switched off, including the flashing lights of the fruit machine in the Full Bar. I was cleaning up the bar when I happened to look up and I saw this misty haze hovering at the fruit machine. She was just a grey mist of a gown and a veil, I think she probably had long hair. I could tell that she was female, slim and small,

about four feet eight inches in height. She was hovering where the door into the Back Bar used to be, which is where the fruit machine now stands; the present entrance was just a blank wall.

I was gobsmacked. I just stood there and stared. She was there for about twenty or thirty seconds before she faded away. I don't think she moved at all but I wouldn't swear to it.

About four months later I saw her in exactly the same place again. By the second time I had got used to the idea and I was more interested to find out what she was doing here. I moved towards her but she just faded away.

I'm told that this was once an ale house where they only sold ale. During that time a young girl died in the upstairs room and although she died from natural causes she now haunts the house as a grey lady.

One of the regulars tells a story which provides another candidate for the grey lady.

In 1995 Ye Olde Severn Stars was under different management. An Australian boy lived here for a while who helped out in the bar and did odd jobs. He had a girlfriend who was a very sensible young lady, not given to fantasies, and after he had lived here for some months she moved in with him. This young lady knew nothing about the history of

☎ 01562 822475

➡ In Coventry Street, off Blackwell Street

⊘ Mon–Sun: 1200–2330

🧍 In summer in garden

🍽 Home-cooked

⛱ Large beer garden

🍺 A Courage pub with a special beer, Enville Ale

ⓘ Modern juke box and occasional live duos

the pub and its reputation of being haunted by a grey lady. She told me that one night, the room became so cold that it woke her up and she sat up in bed to see an elderly lady. This old lady was beckoning to her to follow, but the girl wouldn't and eventually the old lady faded away.

The story goes that the old lady ran the pub for a long time towards the end of the last century. She had a mentally subnormal son who had an accident in the cellars and died. The grey lady is the old woman searching for her son.

☎ **01562 824664**

➜ 95 New Road

⊘ Mon–Sun: 1100–2300

⛾ Bar snacks

🍺 A Banks's pub.

ⓘ Has a juke box.

Corn Exchange

THE IMPORTANCE OF BUYING AND SELLING CORN IN THE 1800S IS ILLUSTRATED BY THE FACT THAT THERE ARE TWO VICTORIAN CORN EXCHANGE BUILDINGS IN KIDDERMINSTER. ONE IS BY THE OLD TOWN HALL, LAW COURTS AND POLICE STATION, THE OTHER IS A PUBLIC HOUSE ALONGSIDE THE MARKET.

Until about 1800 England was able to provide enough grain for its population, but then the home supply was not sufficient and the French wars cut off foreign supplies. The price of bread soared and riots broke out across England. Corn became a political issue and over the next half century various acts were passed to try to improve matters.

Although the Corn Exchange public house was a commercial hotel by 1901, it is assumed that it was originally built as a corn exchange because it is so near to the old market.

It was refurbished towards the end of the 1980's when the two main rooms were knocked into one. Mark Myers became landlord in about 1991 and was told by the previous licensee that out-of-the-ordinary things happened there.

A younger member of the family had seen something when she had slept in a room on the first floor normally used for bed and breakfast. Also, their dog wouldn't go down the stairs into the pub at night.

I was a non-believer and I took all these tales with a pinch of salt until one Sunday evening. Those were the days when you closed on a Sunday afternoon and opened up at 7 pm, so I was alone in the pub about ten or quarter to seven gettting everything ready. I had just put on half-a-dozen switches which gave me the minimum of light. Right on the middle of the pub is a pillar, it must have been put there when the two rooms were knocked into one. I saw a woman standing there, right by the pillar. She was elderly, wearing a cream trouser suit. It all happened so quickly I can't remember any more details but I know that she gave the impression that she was from the 1970's. I blinked, and she was gone.

The locals say that three or four people have seen the apparition. She's known as Mary, she appears on the top floor and is said to be a previous landlady. However, according to the present licensees, Mary appears to have a male friend. Marion and Michael took over the Corn Exchange on 31 March 1998. Marion says:

I knew Jim O'Sullivan who was the licensee here for three years. He was a matter-of-fact bloke and he always said that there was a ghost here. It's very eerie in the evening. From my bedroom to the bathroom I have to go through a kitchen and as I walk through I feel as if someone is watching me.

All kinds of strange things happen. I put things in one place upstairs and they will turn up somewhere stupid. I have found my paperwork in the kitchen and in the bathroom—I would never dream of taking it there. I get really annoyed because I know where I have put things but five or ten minutes later they are not there. The light bulbs keep blowing despite the electrician having checked the wiring loads of times. The juke box keeps going wrong. We have had it checked as much as four or five times in one day but nobody has been able to find the fault and we have recently had a new one. The telephone keeps playing up. We have had the engineers out goodness knows how many times. They have put in a new phone but it's still going wrong now. Someone last night made a telephone call and he was speaking to the person the other end but all she was saying was, 'Hullo! Hullo!'. She couldn't hear him.

We brought two cats with us and their personality changed completely. We did everything we could, but each morning we would find them huddled together under an armchair upstairs. The one cat was very loving but he went beserk and clawed Mick, he would never have done that before. The RSPCA told us they would soon settle down but they never did. In the end we had to give them to the RSPCA. It broke my heart.

On Thursday, 25th of June, I was standing at the bar when someone gave me a push. It was not a little push but a big push. Just after midnight that same day four of us were sitting at the table nearest the bar having a chat. I was sitting with my back to the room and Lisa, who works behind the bar, was opposite me. Suddenly I saw the expression on her face change. She had seen someone walk across the room from right to left in front of the tv screen. She later told me that he was a tallish man, dark-haired, all in black with clothes that looked rather Edwardian. We had closed so it couldn't have been anyone, and Lisa doesn't drink. It spooked her and it really spooked me!

(Note: A female apparition in a 1970's style cream trouser suit was also seen at the Bell, Astwood Bank)

Whittington Inn

NO OTHER INN HAS AS MANY ROMANTIC STORIES AS THIS ONE. IT IS ASSOCIATED WITH DICK WHITTINGTON, LADY JANE GREY, CHARLES II, QUEEN ANNE AND A TERRIBLE MURDER.

The Whittington Inn was the Manor House of the De Whittingtons. Much of the original building still exists which was built by Dick Whittington's grandfather in 1310. Sadly, Dick Whittington came from a well-established family and did not walk to London barefoot but probably rode in on horseback accompanied by a servant. However, the legend is correct in that he did become Lord Mayor of London four times, although not consecutively.

The Inn took part in one of the greatest adventure stories of English history, when, in 1642, the young Charles (later to become Charles II) fled from the battle of Worcester and was in the run for six weeks, with the price of £1,000 on his head, before he escaped to France. A contemporary account states that he 'stayed one night at the Manor House of Whittington on the heath'. Perhaps he hid in one of the two priests' holes uncovered in recent renovations.

Another royal visitor was Queen Anne. It was her custom to have her iron seal fixed upon the front door of houses giving her hospitality and it is still there 'Anne R 1711'. There are only two seals left in England and this is one of them.

In 1430, Lord of the Manor was Humphrey de la Lowe whose daughter married a member of the Grey family. It is said that the tragic Lady Jane Grey spent some of her childhood here. Crowned queen in 1583 when only sixteen, she reigned for ten days before she was sent to the Tower for trial and execution. The ghost of a grey lady, thought to be Lady Jane Grey, is so well-known that a local artist, Robin Jennings, has painted an imaginary scene showing the grey lady in the Whittington Inn and this hangs in the old part of the building.

In the old part of the Inn are six large rings fastened into the ceiling.

SUDDENLY A BIRO... *BURST INTO* flame

From one of these rings, in 1805, William Howe hung his lantern after he had murdered Squire Robins of nearby Dunsley Hall. Howe was a local man and he knew that the Squire would pass through Gibbet Wood on his way home from the fair with a full purse. He robbed him and left him for dead but the Squire managed to crawl home before he died to give the identity of the robber. Howe was arrested at the Whittington Inn, and eventually hung. His was the last corpse in England to be left hanging in chains from a gibbet to deter others (see the Stewponey Hotel, Kinver). The lantern remained on the beam until 1926.

Mary has worked behind the bar since 1976. She says:

All kinds of strange things have happened here. About five times I have been at the sink talking to a customer and suddenly, all the taps have been turned full on.

We had a case of spontaneous combustion. In the old part of the building is a short shelf made from ancient timbers, about two feet long and eighteen inches wide. Nobody was in the bar and the place had been empty for some time, when suddenly a biro, which had been left on this shelf, burst into flame and burned a hole in the woodwork. The shelf has been repaired and sanded down but the mark was so deep that it was impossible to get rid of and the indentation is still there.

We had a dog here called Honey, a Labrador, which absolutely refused to go into certain areas. The cleaners have felt someone touching their shoulders when nobody is there, and the boss who was here in 1976 saw a shadowy figure at the bottom of the bar.

Miss Page was a small child living in the house in the 1970's, and she says that her parents left because of the ghostly footsteps heard pacing the corridor at night. Whether this was Dick Whittington, Lady Jane Grey, King Charles or William Howe nobody knows.

☎ **01384 872110**

➔ In splendid isolation on the A449 about three miles north of Kidderminster

Ⓟ Mon–Sun: All day and evening

Yes

🍴 Bar snacks and restaurant meals

⛱ Beautiful garden includes a large fishpond.

🍺 Banks's, Marston's Pedigree and guest beers

ⓘ Log fires in winter. French Boules is played here, they have two teams and visitors may join in. Although a large pub, has retained a traditional homely ambience. A much publicised inn which featured recently in the *Sunday Mercury* and the *Express and Star*. Mentioned in several books including the *Good Beer Guide*.

KINVER

01384 872835

At the junction of the A449 and A458, west of Stourbridge

Mon–Sun: 1130–1400
1800–2300

Yes

Home-cooked bar meals and snacks

Patio

Owned by Wolverhampton and Dudley Breweries. Facilities for functions. Although called a Hotel, doesn't offer accommodation. Live music is played four nights a week.

Stewponey Hotel

A MILE FROM THE WHITTING-TON INN IS THE STEWPONEY HOTEL WHICH IS TWO OLD INNS COMBINED, THE STEWPONEY AND THE FOLEY ARMS. ALTHOUGH NOW A COMFORTABLE PUBLIC HOUSE, IT WAS ONCE A SINISTER PLACE SET IN WILD AND DESOLATE COUNTRYSIDE. MANY A HIGHWAYMAN SPENT THE NIGHT HERE, DESPITE THE FACT THAT A PARTNER IN CRIME WOULD OFTEN HAVE BEEN HANGING ON THE NEARBY GIBBET. PASSING COACHES WOULD STOP AND PUT DOWN PASSENGERS SO THAT THEY COULD TAKE A TRIP TO VIEW THE GIBBET. IT WAS HERE THAT WILLIAM HOWE'S BODY ROTTED AWAY (SEE THE WHITTINGTON INN, KINVER).

When Queen Anne came to throne in 1702, England's lengthy quarrel with the French was reaching its climax, culminating in the Battle of Blenheim (1704) and England was also involved in the War of the Spanish Succession (1702-1714) where almost the whole of Europe was at each other's throats. According to the Victorian historian and novelist Baring-Gould:

An old soldier in the wars of Queen Anne, a native of the place, settled there when her wars were over and, as was customary with old soldiers, set up an inn near the bridge at the cross roads. He had been quartered at Estepona, in the south of Spain, and thence he had brought a Spanish wife. Partly in honour of her, chiefly in reminis-cence of his old military days, he entitled his inn, "The Estepona Tavern". The Spanish name in English mouths became rapidly transformed into Stewponey.

The inn soon established a reputation as one of the best inns in Staffordshire.

The present licensee, Brian, is sceptical about any ghosts. He says that he came in 1991 and has never seen anything. However, he admits that the old-time regulars say that a white lady has been known to roam the corridors. She is said to be a Spanish woman, nicknamed Estepona. There seems to be no reason why she should haunt the pub as her time at the Stewponey was a happy one.

the Tavern

THE TAVERN IS A VICTORIAN pub, probably built to serve the railway which used to run to Newnham Bridge. The nursery in the centre of the village, down below The Tavern, was once the station. Trains took farm produce into Birmingham and brought out hop-pickers. Engines were refuelled and watered outside the Tavern, when the driver would nip up the steps and into the pub for a couple of pints of home-brewed scrumpy. No doubt some of the passengers did the same—as Lynette discovered.

Everyone will think I'm crazy when they know what I've seen. I've not a lot to tell, really. It was just one of those things.

One autumn a few years ago I was working weekends part-time at the Tavern. I had finished serving the lunches and I was washing the glasses in the small sink downstairs in the restaurant area, when I felt the room get so cold that it made me look up, and there she was. She moved across the room and I said, 'Excuse me, can I help you?'. It wasn't until she floated through the wall that I realised what she was. When you walk you bob up and down but she moved across keeping at exactly the same height.

She had on a funny old dress. She was wearing a bonnet, flattish at the back, with a ribbon under the chin. The front bit was peaked up and also the side bit which came over her face, so that I couldn't see what she looked like. Because I couldn't see her face I don't know how old she was but from her figure she couldn't have been that old. She was slim with a very small waist and a good stature—her back was very straight. The top of her dress went down at the back into a big bow with lots of ribbon, then from the waist it went out and down. The dress stuck out at the front from the waist, not as if she was pregnant but as if she had something inside it, making it stick out. Both of her hands were in this furry muff which she was holding in front of her. The colour was a kind of chocolate brown, both the hat and the dress were the same colour and it was a very nice material with a shine, it looked quite expensive.

She took a route going from the pillar on my left to the kitchen on my right and she must have gone straight through an eight-seater dining table. The pub had not long been redone and the door had been moved about three feet. She went through where the door used to be.

I was so surprised that I pulled a drawer open too far and a glass fell into the sink, where it broke.

Lynette's descripton of the dress is very precise and it would seem to belong to the 1930's. When the present licensee heard this story, he remarked:

In the 1960's the railway embankment outside the Tavern was levelled out and an extension built. The apparition was seen in this new extension and so, as she was obviously from many years ago, she would have been outside. She would have been heading towards the old steps that lead down to the station.

☎ **01584 781331**

Above Station House Garden Centre. Going from Kidderminster, take the first right after the junction of the roads from Kidderminster and Ombersley, then first left

Mon–Sun: 1130–1500 1830–2300

Children welcome, indoor and outdoor play area

Restaurant meals and bar snacks

Garden with play equipment

Free house, with a regular guest ale

ⓘ Reputation for good food and the restaurant looks out over the Worcester-shire countryside.

Talbot Hotel

☎ 01584 781355

Mon–Sat: 1100–1500
1800–2300
Sun: 1100–1500
1900–2230

Allowed 'if well-behaved and on a lead'

Free house with Banks's beers

Seven en suite rooms. Landlady says 'We serve all kinds of food and it's absolutely delicious, we have a reputation for good food. We also pride ourselves on our friendly bar staff'.

THE FRONT DOOR OF THE TALBOT IS AN EASILY RECOGNISABLE LANDMARK ON THE ROAD FROM TENBURY WELLS TO GREAT WITLEY. THE ROAD CURVES SLIGHTLY SO THAT THE IMPOSING DOORWAY SEEMS TO FACE THE TRAFFIC. THE BUILDING IS SEVERAL HUNDRED YEARS OLD AND IT COULD ONCE HAVE BEEN A TOLL HOUSE WHICH WOULD EXPLAIN ITS PROMINENT POSITION.

ROB IS AN ELECTRICIAN WITH A SIDELINE AS A DISC JOCKEY AND AT TWO O'CLOCK ONE AUTUMN MORNING IN THE EARLY 1990'S…

'MY DAUGHTER AND I HAD BEEN DOING A DISCO AT TENBURY AND WE WERE DRIVING BACK TO WORCESTER. AS WE DROVE OVER THE BRIDGE AND HEADED TOWARDS GREAT WITLEY THE HEADLIGHTS ILLUMINATED THE FRONT DOOR OF THE TALBOT AND THERE, ON THE TOP STEP, WAS AN OLD BLOKE WITH A LONG GREY COAT, A BOWLER HAT, A LONG GREY BEARD AND A STERN FACE. HE LOOKED VERY VICTORIAN AND, WHAT IS MORE, YOU COULD SEE THROUGH HIM. WE LOOKED AT HIM THEN WE LOOKED AT EACH OTHER AND WE SAID, "CAN YOU SEE WHAT I CAN SEE?".'

Angel Inn & Posting House

☎ **01386 552046**

 Non-residents:
Mon–Sat: 1000–2300
Sun: 1000–2230

 Allowed when food served

 Bar and restaurant

 Riverside garden

 Whitbread beers on tap

 Accommodation: 16 rooms with two four-poster honeymoon suites. Reputation for good food served in oak-panelled rooms. Three AA stars

DURING THE EIGHTEENTH CENTURY THE ANGEL WAS AN IMPORTANT COACHING INN

patronised by the rich and famous. When the wife of Lord Powys went into labour during a long coach journey, it was The Angel that she chose to produce her son and heir. From time to time mysterious well-dressed strangers would slip in and out of its doors, these would be the gentlemen highwaymen such as the infamous Captain Thomas Dangerfield.

The Angel was also a posting house, where the mail coaches would change horses, collect any post and deposit local mail which would then be distributed by a group of boys. The proprietor in 1932 said that he could remember the post boys, there were seven of them and they slept on straw in a row of little cubicles above the stables, 'just like coffins'.

The present owner/manager, Juan Mendez, says he can sometimes feel a very peculiar cold draft in the corridor next to the restaurant. He adds:

I was in the bar with one of my local customers about two years ago and he said, 'How many guests have you got tonight?'. I told him that we were empty that night. We carried on drinking and then we could hear a man's heavy footsteps upstairs in the old part of the building. The customer remarked, 'I thought you said there were no guests, there is someone upstairs'. We rushed upstairs and switched on the lights but there was nobody about.

Many people seem to have seen a ghost in the restaurant, they all describe him as a large man, very well-dressed.

One of his customers, Gerald Wrigley, spent many a weekend there with his wife, Joyce. Unfortunately, Gerald has recently passed away but Joyce describes an incident which occurred one Good Friday evening.

We often stayed at the Angel Inn at Pershore and in 1994, we decided to spend our Easter holiday there. The dining room was quite full on the Friday evening. We sat in the bay on the left hand side and I was facing Gerald with my back to the fireplace. Suddenly, he looked up and saw the figure of a man standing in front of the fireplace. His first thought was that it was Mr Mendez and he said to himself, 'That's a funny place to stand'. It was between two tables which were quite close and there wasn't really room for anyone to stand there. Three ladies were at the one table and I forget who was at the other. When he told me I turned round to look but I couldn't see anything. I said, 'Where is it?' but evidently it had faded away.

Then it reappeared. My husband said, with his hand over his mouth', 'There it is again, look!' but I didn't like to keep turning round. People would start staring. Apparently, it faded away and reappeared yet again. He saw it three times quite clearly in about two minutes.

I asked Gerald to describe it. My husband was an ex-naval man and he said that the figure was wearing an old naval square rig uniform, a dark blue donkey jacket with buttons. When I pressed for more details, he added, 'You know, you've seen it in old war films'. I also asked him about the hat but I can't remember what he said.

He didn't seem at all surprised. I asked him how he felt now that he had seen a ghost and he replied, 'I feel privileged'.

We told Mr Mendez and he said that the ghost had been seen before in that same spot. We had already heard that the hotel was subject to footsteps.

☎ **01527 62180**

 Mon–Sun: 1200–2100

 Bar menu

 Scottish and Newcastle products

ⓘ A disco is held on Fridays for students

the Limelight

IN A DARK CORNER OF THE KINGFISHER SHOPPING CENTRE, near the top of the escalators to the 'bus station, is the entrance is to the Limelight public house. It was among the first section of the shopping centre to be opened in 1973.

Marjorie Shakespeare has now retired but in 1989 she was a cleaner at the Limelight, starting work at 7 o'clock each week day morning.

I went in one morning and, as usual, there were no lights were on and it was pitch dark. As soon as I opened the door I noticed a mouldy smell. I thought, 'I have left some beer drying out somewhere, I must find it when I get started'.

I had 60 seconds to get from the door to the back of the counter to turn the alarm off, which I did. There was a crate in the middle of the bar and I tripped over it which left me short of breath, and as I suffer from asthma I had to sit down. I was sitting there and I still hadn't put the lights on, when all of a sudden, this kind of see-through image came floating across the bar.

When I first saw it, I was going to say, 'You're up, Paul!' the movement of it was so real. It was the shape of a small man in a bowler hat, although I couldn't see any detail. It was all white, see-through, rather like a handful of frog's spawn. It wasn't long, it was more oval and it floated up and down through the air, about four or five feet off the floor. It floated over the bar, came all across the room and went out through the open doorway. I always thought that spirits could go through walls but this one went through the door. I thought, 'How beautiful, how lovely!' and I thought, 'I have seen a spirit!'

People are sceptical but I know what I saw. It had such an effect on me that a week later I went and found a church that I was comfortable in and I have gone ever since.

Paul and Martine live in the flat above the premises. Paul has been the licensee since 1983 but has only lived there for the past six years. He says he can remember Mrs Shakespeare but he didn't hear about the incident she describes.

Martine told the following story, with Paul listening and adding a little information here and there.

There is definitely something here, there is so much happening. All the staff have experienced something but it's nothing frightening. If I thought that there was anything unpleasant I wouldn't be staying here with my three kids. The incidents are the sort of things a mischievous small child would do. When the barmen are bending down in the bar they feel their bottom pinched. It happened to me when I was emptying the dishwasher. When someone's working in the kitchen they can hear their name called, it sounds as if the caller is hiding. They come out and say to the barman, 'What do you want?' and the barman says, 'What do you mean?'. One night, when I was locking up on my own, I bent down behind the bar and somebody shouted, 'Boo!' and my hair was pulled across my face.

The gas cylinders are switched off—we change the barrel and do everything properly but then the beer's not working.

I saw the

The lights dim a lot and we have power surges; last Saturday the electricity went off three times, which meant that there were no lights and all the machines went off. All the time things disappear and come back in strange places, it could be the kids but they swear black and blue its not them. Sometimes things completely disappear such as the Sky remote control. We still haven't found that.

It happens to all of us, even the customers. A customer who sat in the bar has seen a glass lift up and turn over in the mirror. Little things happen that don't have any explanation.

We think it's a small boy, not long after we had moved here our son came into us one night—he was six—and he said that the telly kept changing channels. He said, 'It's not me, it's the little boy who sits on the bed with me'.

One night, I sat up in bed and I was sure that I saw the shadow of a small child on the wall. I wouldn't go to sleep. Paul got out of bed and had a look round but he couldn't find anything and the three children were fast asleep.

Len, the Assistant Manager, says:

Let me begin by telling you a story. About eighteen years ago, before I was married, I had a girlfriend who lived in Webheath and I would run from Batchley and back again almost every day to see her. I was going along Downsell Road, and was going round the corner, turning into Tynsall Avenue, when a chap wearing a Levi jacket and jeans jumped out at me and shouted 'Wargh!'. I was startled and ran on for a second or two, then I

thought, 'Hang on, I recognise that face!'. The features were those of my brother who had died in a car accident twelve months previously. I stopped and looked round but no-one was there. It would have been very difficult for someone to get out of sight so quickly. That is just the sort of thing he would have done, had he been alive. It was really weird.

Anyway, I told this story in the Sticky Wicket, and just as I said, 'Wargh!' a large display of about fifty Pils lager bottles which were stacked in a pyramid all collapsed. The display was quite stable and it had been there for some months. About twelve months ago I started working in the Limelight and I told the same story there. As I came to 'Wargh!' the lights flashed and the

till went off. It took Martine ages to get the till working again.

Most of the strange happenings in the Limelight, which Paul has mentioned, have also happened to me. The lights keep dipping, and I was bending down when someone gave my bottom a hard tap.

I remember that once, I filled the barrels in the morning, opened the pub up and pulled about ten pints. All of a sudden, the other barman said, 'The barrel's gone'. I thought the gas must have run out so I went down the cellar to have a look. The gas was full but the barrel was switched off. Someone had pulled down the handle which operated the barrel. I was the only one who had been down there and that was when I filled the barrels first thing in the morning.

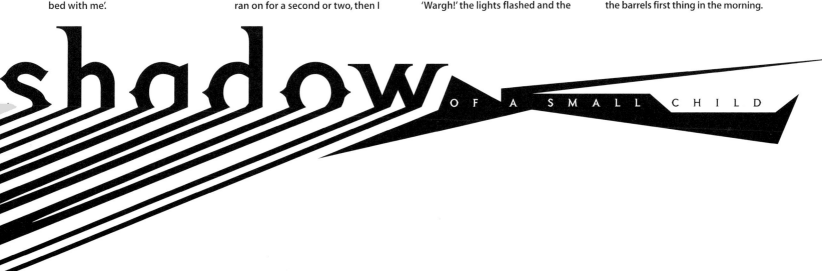

shadow OF A SMALL CHILD

Old Rectory

PARTS OF THE OLD RECTORY ARE THOUGHT TO BE A THOUSAND YEARS OLD. IT WAS ONCE THE HOME OF THE HUBAND FAMILY, BEFORE SIR JOHN HUBAND MOVED ACROSS THE ROAD TO IPSLEY COURT AND ALLOWED THE RECTORS OF IPSLEY TO LIVE IN HIS OLD HOME RENT FREE.

The Old Rectory was converted into a hotel by Tony Moore in the 1960's who regarded their resident ghost with great affection and called him 'Charlie'.

☎ 01527 523000

➜ In Ipsley Lane which is almost opposite Church Lane. Ipsley is east Redditch and signposted from the Warwick Highway

⊞ Large gardens

ⓘ Accommodation: Ten rooms. Has been awarded three crowns, highly commended.

It appears in a large room at the front of the house. You can see from the pointed window that this room was once a chapel, and a priest's hiding hole runs from here to rooms on two other floors.

When we first moved into this house in the 1960's our three small children used to sleep in the chapel room. My eldest son, Edward, was four. One morning, Edward said, 'Who was that who came into our bedroom during the night? He came over and looked at me in my bed, then he went over to the cot and looked at the baby, then he came over here and looked at Jonathon. Then— he just went!'. We asked Edward to describe him. 'He had a thing on his head', he said, showing us how it came up to a point, 'then it went straight down to the ground'. Isn't that, for a four year old, a perfect description of a monk's habit?

The vicar from Bridbrooke (in Warwick) and his wife were once staying here and they said somebody had crossed the room during the night but they hadn't heard the door open, nor the shuffling of feet on the carpet.

A year or two later another couple sleeping in this room asked us 'Is our room haunted?'. We hadn't mentioned the subject, so the idea came from them, not from us. It seemed that the husband had apparently got up during the night, rather surprising the wife because he didn't do that at home. The next night he seemed to get out of bed again and walk across the room. This time, she sat up in bed and there was her husband fast asleep—he hadn't budged! In retrospect she realised that there had been no noise of footsteps walking over the carpet.

The present manager, Greg Underwood, adds:

Some time later, two children were sleeping in that room while wedding celebrations were in progress downstairs. At 12.30 pm they both appeared on the main staircase asking who was the man who had walked into their room, walked all around the walls and then left. All the wedding guests were downstairs—nobody but the children were upstairs.

REDDITCH, IPSLEY

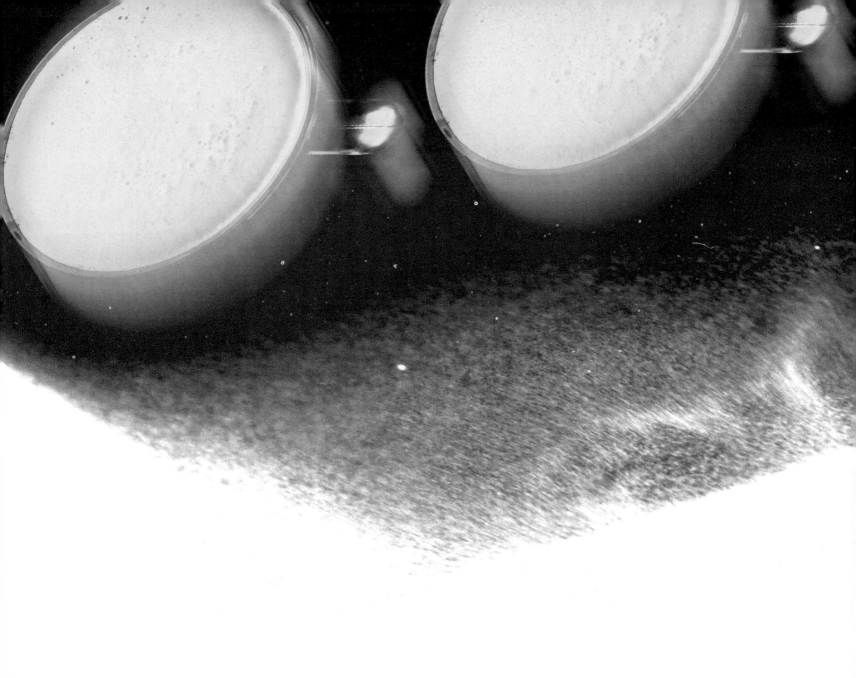

Manchester Inn

THE MANCHESTER INN WAS REGISTERED AS AN INN IN 1858 BUT PROBABLY BUILT BEFORE THEN. NO-ONE KNOWS EXACTLY HOW OLD IT IS, NOR HOW IT CAME BY ITS NAME AND CAN ONLY ASSUME THAT AN EARLY LANDLORD MOST LIKELY CAME FROM MANCHESTER.

The story is told by one of the regulars of the Manchester Inn. Those concerned find the episode very embarrassing and therefore no names have been given.

Two friends of mine, a married couple in their late fifties, live with their two daughters in Romsley. They have a routine on a Saturday evening of travelling on a certain visit and then ending the evening at their local, the Manchester Inn at Romsley. The return journey from their visit to the Manchester takes them past their own house. On this occasion, the wife, who is teetotal, was driving.

Now we come to the interesting bit, when on a Saturday evening sometime in the spring of 1995, my two friends were driving past their house towards their local, when they noticed their daughter coming out of the front door, about to get into her car. At that point the husband asked his wife, who had also seen her daughter, to slow down and go around the village green (which was situated approximately 150 yards from their house) so that they could collect her. As they arrived on the forecourt of their house (which would have taken two minutes at the most) they were astonished to find both car and daughter gone. Considering the openness of the location and the time it took to return to their home, the husband and wife were baffled that she could have disappeared without them seeing her. The couple continued on to their original destination situated approximately a quarter of a mile down the road. During the short journey a conversation took place regarding the whereabouts of their daughter. The conclusion was that she must have changed her plans, travelled in the opposite direction and would not be joining them—which was unusual for a Saturday night.

On arriving at the pub both husband and wife were further perplexed to discover their daughter's car on the car park. They parked alongside and on entering the Lounge they were amazed to see their daughter sitting in company, her glass three-quarters empty. The husband enquired as to how she had got there so quickly without passing them. She replied with equal astonishment that she had been there for thirty-five minutes, a story corroborated by the company she was with and the bar staff. These events remained the topic of discussion for the rest of the evening.

My friends remain puzzled to this day by this odd sequence of events.

☎ **01562 710242**

→ On the B4551 one mile south of Romsley

🕐 Mon–Sat: 1130–1430
1700–2300
Sun: 1130–1430
1700–2230

 Home-cooked

 Yes

🍺 Usually a guest beer

ⓘ Delightfully situated on the edge of the Waseley Hills Country Park. Featured in *Pub Walks in Worcestershire*

☎ **01386 871300**

→ Situated on the B439
near Salford Priors

🕐 Non-residents:
Mon–Sun: normal

🧍 Yes

🍴 2 AA rosettes for food

⛽ Yes

ℹ️ This is a 3-star Charter
Hotel with 34 en suite
rooms. During December
murder evenings and
weekends are available
for special parties

SALFORD PRIORS

Salford Hall

SALFORD HALL IS A LARGE STONE ELIZABETHAN HOUSE WITH UNUSUALLY-SHAPED GABLES, WITH THE DATE 1602 OVER THE PORCH BUT BUILT SOME TIME BEFORE THEN FOR THE ABBOTS OF EVESHAM.

Details of the following ghost story are published in a little booklet of sixty pages available from the Hall.

From 1807 to 1829 Salford Hall was occupied by a community of Benedictine nuns who had been forced to leave Cambrai because of the French Revolution. They converted the Hall into a girls' boarding school.

In 1815, a coach drew up at the front door and a man bundled two little girls inside with great haste. He gave the mother superior enough money to keep the girls at school until they were eighteen, when a certain advertisement was to be placed in The Times. He rushed away and no-one saw him again. The girls were two little Americans, Evra, aged 11, and Wyom, aged 13. They were very happy at the school, the nuns treating them as if they were their own children. On Wyom's eighteenth birthday an advertisement was placed in The Times as instructed. A letter arrived telling Wyom to go to a certain house in London, and tearful good-byes were said. Although Wyom promised to write, the weeks passed and no word came. Then Evra began walking in her sleep, and she confided to the abbess that she had dreamt that her sister was being held prisoner.

The abbess discovered that the address to which Wyom had gone did not exist. The police were notified and eventually, thanks to the presence of mind of a young doctor, Wyom was found in a house in Buckingham, suffering from stab wounds. Her guardian's son had kidnapped her and was trying to get his hands on her money. He was in a state of hysteria and said that he had been driven crazy by the ghost of a girl who appeared every night and would not leave him alone.

Evra had fallen ill with grief and had died, but Wyom recovered and married the doctor who was responsible for her rescue. Eleven years later their daughter began school at Salford Hall.

We do not know what apparitions walked the corridors of Salford Hall for the next 150 years, but Sally, the Hotel Director, knows of an incident which occurred just after the Hotel opened in 1989:

The husband of one of our members of staff, Paul, came early one morning and happened to ask us what a priest was doing at the hotel. There was no priest staying here. We all laughed and told him to take more water with it next time. A short time later two ladies arrived who were the only ones in the hotel. They wanted to know where the wedding was, because they had seen a priest walking purposefully along the hallway. They described a figure which was just as Paul had seen it.

Somerset House

☎ **01384 394498**

→ Situated just off the Stourbridge ring road which is signposted Bridgnorth and Wollaston

🕐 Mon–Sat: 1200–2300
Sun: 1200–2230

🍴 Outside benches

🍺 A Banks's pub

ⓘ Live disco is held on Saturday evenings

SOMERSET HOUSE WAS LISTED
in 1841 as a Public House and Tavern. It was therefore a place of some importance, selling various liquors and offering accommodation to travellers. Public houses in the early 1800s sometimes offered funeral services and Somerset House was apparently one of them, one of the first landlords had a secondary career, he used to make the village coffins in the back yard. This is not the only reason why Somerset House has acquired a sinister reputation. Strange things happen here. If you place a pint mug of lager against a certain wall, it sticks there. John Selwyn, the Licensee, will perform this trick on request, grabbing any drink which happens to be handy and ignoring the owner's protests. Birmingham University have investigated this phenomenon and believe the cause to be a fine layer of tar and nicotine on the wallpaper. However, this is not the only bizarre occurrence. John Selwyn says:

When you are siting in the pub on your own you can hear things. You can hear the loft boards going up and down as if someone is walking across them, and doors creaking open and closing again. Three or four times over the past few years the CO2 gas has been turned off in the cellar. It takes quite a strong hand to turn it off, it's not something that could happen by accident.

You often feel as if someone is watching you, but I am sure that whatever-it-is wouldn't hurt you. I have never been frightened. I often work here on my own until midnight and you wouldn't catch me doing that if I felt there was any chance of coming face to face with a spook.

IF YOU PLACE A PINT MUG OF LAGER AGAINST A CERTAIN WALL IT STICKS THERE

01384 395112

 The ring road end of
Worcester Street

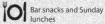 Mon–Sat: 1000–2300
Sun: 1200–2230

 Bar snacks and Sunday
lunches

 Yes

 Guest beers

ⓘ Owned by Avebury Taverns

his HEAD was missing

Waggon and Horses

THE LICENSEE of the Waggon and Horses in 1860 was a Mr Edward Jones, and he complained bitterly that his trade was being affected by various apparitions appearing on the footpath, known as Gibbet Gullet, which ran past his public house. His complaints reached the ears of Lord Lyttleton who set up an enquiry. Witnesses were produced who testified to three ghosts. Two apparitions were young men who made horrible noises and were naked except for their 'breach clouts'. The third was older and fully clothed except that his head was missing.

It was thought that these were the deceased members of the Walker family. John Walker, a court bum-bailiff, had been murdered by his two sons. The sons had been executed at Shrewsbury. John Walker's body had been given to a local surgeon for anatomical study whereas the two sons had been hung from a gibbet, probably at the end of the gullet.

The present licensee, Mr N Salisbury, has been at the Waggon and Horses for three years and nothing strange has occurred so far but he will let everyone know if he is accosted by any naked or headless ghosts.

STOURBRIDGE

Bridge Inn

THE BRIDGE INN IS ONE OF THE OLDEST PUBS IN BRITAIN, DATING BACK TO 1670. BENEATH THE PUB IS A SECONDARY CELLAR WHICH IS NOW BLOCKED UP BUT IS THOUGHT TO BE THE ENTRANCE TO A TUNNEL LEADING TO THE RIVER STOUR. THE OLD TIMERS SAY THAT THE TUNNEL WAS USED FOR SMUGGLING PORT. THEY ALSO SAY THAT THE PUB HAS THE REPUTATION OF BEING HAUNTED.

Landlady Jo Sais left the pub in 1987 and she comments:

I can't explain it, but I had a strange feeling about the two upstairs bedrooms. I wouldn't go in there at first and slept downstairs in the living room, but then when all our furniture arrived I had to sleep up there. But I never liked it. I have never felt that way about any of the other pubs I've lived in.

George and Kath Barber were licensees for fifteen years. George had been a licensee for many years and he said that nowhere else did he encounter strange events similar to that at the Bridge Inn.

According to Mike Pryce of the *Worcester Evening News*, 28th June, 1978:

'The Barbers had been at the Bridge for about three years before anything happened. It was a cold winter's night and the last customers had long since left. The fires were damped down and the bars were silent. George had already gone upstairs to bed, falling into a deep sleep almost as soon as his head hit the pillow. Downstairs, Kath was making a final check on door locks and light switches.

'She flicked a switch and plunged the bars into darkness before turning to go down the narrow passageway which led to the bottom of the staircase. Halfway along the passage was a telephone and as Kath passed she was aware of someone standing by it. She carried on for a few steps, thinking, absentmindedly, that it was their youngest daughter, Mal. "C'mon Mal, let's go to bed", she said wearily. Then suddenly Kath remembered—and looked around. Mal was in bed. Instead of her daughter, standing a few feet away was a woman in a pink crinoline dress. She remained by the phone, motionless, as Kath stared for a few seconds, paralysed by surprise, before dashing upstairs.

'George was still fast asleep and when she told him of her experience the next morning he laughed. However, something was beginning to click into place. Across the corridor from the phone was a door leading down to the pub cellar. Now although George regularly went into the cellar to deal with the beer barrels, neither the Barber's golden retriever dog, Ringo, nor their cat would set a foot even on the cellar steps. Both refused to have anything to do with the room.

'A few months passed and Kath remained convinced that she really had seen something out of the ordinary that night, while George remained sceptical. Then one evening he changed his mind.

'The Barbers were both watching television in their room at the back of the pub when the door to the bar counter opened and into the room drifted The Crinolined Lady. As she passed in front of the television Kath looked at her husband's face which was a picture of disbelief. The dog, which had been asleep, leapt to his feet and his hackles stood stiff as a hedgehog, but he didn't bark or move to attack the apparition.

'Slowly the Crinolined Lady passed through the room and at the opposite end a door into the kitchen opened and she disappeared as swiftly as she had arrived. Neither the kitchen nor the bar door closed behind her. "Perhaps you'll believe me now" Kath exclaimed to her husband.

'Shortly afterwards planned alterations to the pub began and the narrow corridor disappeared. The cellar remained but it was much improved and the dog and cat would go down there without hesitation. That was the last anyone has seen of the Crinolined Lady.'

Mike Pryce was too hasty in his last comment. The present licensee is Mr Lovelock and since he took over in July

It was a cold winter's night

☎ **01299 87745**

→ Situated where bridge crosses river

◔ Mon–Sun:
Summer: 1100–2300
Winter: 1100–1500
1900–2300

ẙ Yes

⧓◍ Home-cooked, barbecues during summer

☰ Yes

ⓘ Owned by Albion Leisure

1997, three strange incidents have occurred.

Obviously, our living accommodation is on the third floor. We were lying in bed and at about two am the bedroom door opened. Now, this door really sticks and you have to push it hard to open it. Because of the slope of the building, the door fell back and banged. We thought it was our five-year old son, so I got out of bed and looked in my son's bedroom but he was fast asleep. My daughter was asleep too. It frightened the wife but, to be honest, I thought nothing of it.

Four or five days later we were serving on the bar in the lunch time—no problem. Then the barmaid came in and said what's the matter with the Worthingtons? It won't pour. I went down the cellar and both gas bottles were turned off as well as the actual barrel to the wall. I know for certain that no-one went down the cellar.

About a week later I was working in the bar late at night. Some people had stayed on, talking, after I had locked up so I let them out of the side door. While I was doing this I had the feeling that somebody was watching me. I returned to the bar and was tidying up when to my amazement I saw this lady walk the full length of the bar. I saw her as clearly as abc. She appeared at the bottom end of the bar and went all the way through it, into the new part of the building. She didn't walk, she glided across and she didn't look at me. She was in her 30's or 40's, tall, with long dark curly hair and she was wearing a creamy-white Victorian costume. It came up under the breast, and flared out from the waist. I could only see her top half - the top three feet - because I was behind the bar. When I had got over my surprise I searched the building but of course, nobody was about.

☎ 01789 764634

→ Dominates the A422
Stratford/Alcester Road
about a mile from
Stratford

Non-residents:
Mon–Sun: 1200–1500
1730–2300

Home-cooked restaurant
and bar meals

Four acres of garden.
Magnificent views
from patio

ⓘ Accommodation: 13 en
suite rooms with Sky
television. Occasionally
live music. A refurbished
sixteenth century
coaching inn with a
reputation for good
food. Awarded 3 crowns

the Stag

TWENTY YEARS AGO John Hunt was a teenager who, from time to time, enjoyed a quiet drink at The Stag. He was fascinated by its history, by the huge old court room, fifty feet long and thirty feet in height with a gallery all round and the remains of the local lock-up at one end. He was intrigued by the large archway running through the centre of the building through which tired horses pulled heavy coaches. He never dreamed that one day he would be the owner.

In renovating the building, John has had to make some changes, but has preserved as much as possible. The archway had been made into a dining room but the old stonework remains. The court room has had to be partitioned off and the gallery converted into bedrooms, but on the first floor he has revealed a window frame which could be late medieval, and one of the doors in the corridor is the old heavily-studded cell door, with its tiny barred window.

John says that local criminals were tried in the court by the circuit judge, and if they were found guilty they were put in the cell and, it is thought, hung at Billesley cross roads. He continues:

Folklore has it that one young man was hung on midsummer day and almost every year since then, on that day, his mother his put in an appearance in the gardens.

On midsummer day of June 1997, one of our guests was staying in the old stables which have now been converted into bedrooms. She checked in at about a quarter to six and she came in and said, 'Where is that little old lady staying?' We asked her what she meant. She said, 'The one I have just had a conversation with in the car park'. We told her that no little old lady was staying here. The lady had said to her, among other things, 'I will see you in the bar' but no little old lady arrived. This hotel is a long way from any housing, there is no way a little old lady could have walked here, and she definitely didn't come by car. Nobody came into the restaurant, nothing. We asked our guest to describe the old lady and she said that she wasn't very well dressed.

John thinks they may also have a second entity.

I have been in this bar on my own when I have heard someone walk straight down the centre of the bar above us. This is not possible, as it's a void. A customer was with me and he said, 'What the hell is that?'. It was a man's footsteps, heavy and slow. The interesting thing is that one of the bedrooms extends over a corner of the bar and several people have remarked upon a cold spot in this bedroom. Three years ago a lady came here who said she was psychic. She went up and spent two hours in the room. She said that one of Cromwell's officers was in this bedroom, he had been injured at the battle of Worcester and he managed to reach here but died when he got here. She said he likes being here, he is very happy and wants to stay here. He never gives us any trouble, he is never a problem.

So much interest has been shown in the ghosts at the Stag, particularly in the elderly lady, that John is allowing any interested persons to stay in the car park overnight on midsummer evening of 1998, providing they get in touch with him beforehand. He says, 'They can sleep in their cars if they want to'.

STRATFORD - REDHILL

STRATFORD-UPON-AVON

Falcon Hotel

SHAKESPEARE'S OLD GRAMMAR SCHOOL STILL STANDS NEAR THE GUILD

Chapel in Stratford. His memories of it do not seem to have been pleasant. In *As you like it* he refers to 'the whining schoolboy ... creeping like a snail/ Unwillingly to school, and in *Richard III*, he writes 'Thy school-days frightful, desperate, wild and furious'. However, he no doubt compensated for his hours of misery in later years at the Falcon Hotel, which is almost opposite the grammar school. The Falcon dates back to the fifteenth century, when it was a single dwelling house but for three hundred years, probably until the beginning of this century, it was divided into three separate houses. Number one was probably always a hostelry of some kind.

Room 307 is one of the splendid rooms which is popular with honeymoon couples, having a large four poster bed. Very occasionally, the happy couple have been joined by a white lady.

The manager, Denis Woodhams, says that he has no idea who this could be as the history of the Falcon has been relatively trouble free, however:

It always appears at exactly 4.30 am. First of all the room goes very cold, Then, according to those who have seen it, a white female form appears to be sitting on the bed, and is without colour, so that it is white from head to toe. She has long hair and a night-dress or long gown which would probably reach the floor. She's quite clearly defined so that those who see her reckon her to be in her early thirties.

The pattern is much the same each time; the wife wakes up, sees the ghost, lets out a yell and rouses her husband. The ghost has gone by the time the husband has opened his eyes properly.

Each time, the wife has come down to the reception desk in the morning and, with an expression of disbelief, has confided, 'I had a peculiar experience last night ...'

Honeymoon couples can rest assured that they can sleep here undisturbed, as the apparition has only put in a brief appearance four times during the last fourteen years.

 01789 279953

 In Chapel Street, almost opposite the Guild Chapel

Children welcome and under-sixteens are free when sharing room with an adult

 The Oak Bar was licensed in 1628 and is one of the oldest in Stratford. Twenty of the seventy-three en suite bedrooms are in the original sixteenth-century inn

STRATFORD-UPON-AVON

☎ **01527 852045**

➡ On the island in Studley centre

 Mon–Sat: 1200–2300
Sun: 1200–2230

👤 Yes

🍴 A variety of home-cooked food is served all day

🌲 Small beer garden

🍺 Guest ales

 One of the 'Vintage Inns' chain which aims to preserve traditional qualities. Specialises in traditional British fare. Runs special appropriate menus on saints' days and other special days eg poets' days, Burns' day, etc. Special facilities for disabled.

Barley Mow

THE BARLEY MOW IS PARTLY HALF-TIMBERED AND COULD BE AS MUCH AS 700 YEARS OLD. IT STANDS IN THE CENTRE OF STUDLEY ON THE OLD ROMAN ROAD, RYKNILD STREET. THE LARGE PLATE GLASS WINDOW WHICH FACES THE ISLAND FILLS IN THE ARCHWAY THROUGH WHICH HORSES AND COACHES ONCE PASSED TO ENTER THE INN. ACROSS THE ROAD FROM THE CAR PARK, BEHIND WHAT IS NOW A GARAGE, A LARGE PRIORY ONCE STOOD. UNTIL THE LATE NINETEENTH CENTURY THERE WAS A BREWHOUSE AT THE EASTERN END OF THE BARLEY MOW.

This inn was a favourite of John Wesley, the founder of the Wesleyan Methodist Church, who broke long journeys twice to stay there. A more recent occasional visitor is Dr Ray Shaw, a local history enthusiast. According to Ray:

The Barley Mow is almost certainly Studley's oldest pub and is reputed to have been the brew-house for the Augustinian Priory which was nearby. The connection with monks is interesting as the history of Studley Priory is well documented. If the accounts are accurate then it seems that the monks were far more likely to be flat on their backs in the brew-house than on their knees in the Church. The history states that the Priory was 'mismanaged' and that there was continual discord with the Church of Worcester.

In 1364, a visiting Prior of Worcester was met by 'bows and weapons' when he came to admonish the monks for 'religious laxity' and not observing the rule of silence. The monks gave way when threatened with excommunication. During the reign of Henry VI (1421-61) the Bishop of Worcester received a petition stating that the Prior of Studley was maintaining a para-mour, one Joan Greene, at Skilts, and thus 'impoverishing' the monastery. The Priory met its end along with most others in 1538 in Henry VIII's Reformation.

One evening, a verse written up on the blackboard caught my eye which mentioned 'strange shadows'. I thought 'strange shadows?' and recalled the monk story. A chat to the locals gave me a name or two and I managed to track down a reluctant informant who once worked in the kitchen; he said that when he was working in there he saw a monk walk past him. These monastic manifesta-tions have been confirmed by one of the bar staff who works in the bar alone in the afternoon.

Simon Campbell, the Assistant Manager, was a staunch disbeliever before he came. Now he admits that there is something strange about the pub, in fact, he himself once saw something that he could not explain.

The previous landlord told me when he left that there was a resident spook here but he didn't know much about it and had never seen it himself. He said that the locals had mentioned some kind of presence.

I once saw something for which I have no explanation and which is very difficult to describe. I live in a flat upstairs and one night, I locked up, alarmed the building and went upstairs. I was doing something in my room when I looked up and saw a dark shape in my doorway. It was the silhouette of a woman and I could just make out that she had long blond hair. I was so certain that

it was somebody that I spoke to her but when I moved towards the doorway nobody was there. It didn't occur to me that it could have been a ghost until I was thinking about it afterwards. However, I'm a bit wary. It's often midnight before I get to bed, so if I see something strange, could it be that my eyes were playing tricks because I was tired?

During the night, this week, while I was lying upstairs I could hear what sounded like chairs moving downstairs. The building has alarms and it is censored but nothing went off. These alarms do work because we have them checked regularly.

I'm told that the apparition is busiest just before November 5th each year and I must admit that one or two strange things happened at that time last year. One of our waitresses was taking a meal into the dining room when she heard someone behind her saying, 'I'm watching you!'. She turned round but nobody was there, and all night she felt as if someone was watching her. She said that it gave her the eebeejeebies.

About the same time, a couple of guests said that they had given an order for coffee and it had not arrived. When I asked them to describe the waitress that they gave the order to, there was no-one of that description on the staff. I wouldn't have thought twice about this incident except that exactly the same thing happened again a few days later. It has never happened before or since.

There are tunnels that are said to run between the Priory and the Barley Mow. They are blocked off but haven't been filled in. I am told that Bob of 'Bob's Wines', which is just up the Redditch Road, has seen them. Some people thought the apparition might be associated with that. Others thought it might be a landlady who died on the premises. Then there was a nasty accident here in 1883 when the barman, Walter Hollis, drowned in a vat of beer. Could his wife or girlfriend come looking for him?

I don't mind the apparition at all. It doesn't do any harm and it provides a talking point for the regulars.

Even more difficult to rationalise is the experience of Pat, who visits the Barley Mow with her husband and daughter two or three times a week.

It's a lovely, happy atmosphere here. I wouldn't come otherwise. There's just one area I don't like. Whenever I sit at the round table in the bay window opposite the bar, I feel peculiar. The atmosphere is oppressive and my head aches, as if I have a migraine coming on. Once or twice I've had to sit there when the bar is full and I have had to refuse any food, I always say, 'I can't eat here!'. First of all, I put it down to the lights, I thought the lighting didn't suit me. Then, on two occasions in mid-afternoon, when I have sat there, I have looked across to the bar and seen two strange people, a man and a woman. I can see the chap most clearly, he is all in black with a frock coat, gaiters, buckled shoes and a tricorn hat. He's aged about twenty-four, medium height, thick-set with a round, pleasant-looking face. He's standing there, sideways on to the bar, with a lady. I can't see her clearly, she's just a white shape but I can make out that her dress is very pretty, of muslin or some other fine fabric. She doesn't look to me like one of the lower classes, I would say that she has a much higher status than a serving wench. They stand as if they are having a conversation and I would say they are very comfortable in each other's company, perhaps on intimate terms. They stay there without moving and I can see them for about twenty minutes before they disappear. It's a happy scene and I don't know why I feel so uncomfortable about it.

A final comment comes from the manager, Darrall Bebbington, who has taken an interest in the history of the building.

Where Pat saw her two ghosts is the original part of the pub. There is a beam in a room above which is dated 1584. It would have been next door to the old brewery, which stood between the end of the central bar and the area in front of the plate glass window.

The tricorn could be explained by the fact that the old maltsters traditionally wore a three-cornered hat.

Sometimes, when I lock up at night, I feel that I am not alone. This is a large place to close up and I have to walk the length of the pub with only the street lights outside to guide me, but I never feel afraid. I am sure that if there is anything here, it is quite friendly.

ne was watching

☎ **01905 345602**

→ Exit the M5 at junction 6.
Take the Evesham road
and turn left at the first
island.

⊘ Mon–Sun: 1200–1500
1800–2300

Yes

⦿ Cooked personally by
landlady

⛽ Yes

☕ A Banks's pub

a terrible and grisly MURDER

IBBERTON (NEAR WORCESTER)

Speed *the* Plough

NO-ONE VISITING THIS PRETTY LITTLE COUNTRY PUB WOULD GUESS THAT IT WAS ONCE INVOLVED IN A TERRIBLE AND GRISLY MURDER. A TINY ROOM ONCE KNOWN AS 'THE SNUG' HAS NOW BEEN COMBINED WITH A LARGER AREA TO FORM A BILLIARD ROOM BUT IT WAS HERE, IN 1806, THAT FIVE EMINENT PARISHIONERS PLANNED TO MURDER THE LOCAL CLERGYMAN. THEY HUDDLED ROUND THE TINY TABLE, DRINKING WITH THEIR LEFT HANDS ONLY WHICH, TRADITIONALLY, LEFT THEIR SWORD HANDS FREE. THE INTENDED VICTIM WAS THE RECTOR OF ODDINGLEY, WHO HAD MADE HIMSELF UNPOPULAR BY HIS RUTHLESS COLLECTION OF TYTHES. THE RINGLEADER WAS CAPTAIN EVANS OF CHURCH FARM, ODDINGLEY; ALSO INVOLVED WERE THOMAS CLEWS OF NETHERTON FARM, AND JOSEPH TAYLOR.

The five men were much too respectable to perform the deed themselves, and so they hired a carpenter and wheelwright from Droitwich, Richard Heming. His thoroughness is almost admirable, first he battered his victim to death, then he shot him, then he set fire to his clothing. Unfortunately, the whole process took so long that he was disturbed by two men from Worcester out for a walk. Heming ran into Trench woods, then later skulked round Church farm and Netherton farm and finally hid in Netherton barn. There, the five conspirators met him, ostensibly to sort things out, but Joseph Taylor lost his temper and killed him. Heming was buried in a corner of the barn, where he lay until 1830, when the barn was demolished. By a strange quirk of fate, the demolition contractor was Heming's brother-in-law. By that time both Evans and Taylor were dead, and current law said that if the principal in a murder was dead, the accessories could refuse to plead, so the other three men were never brought to justice. Clews became licensee of the Fir Tree Inn at Dunhampstead in about 1906. The Rev Parker is buried just inside and on the left of the gate to Oddingley Church.

The main part of the building goes back to 1675 and was originally known as God Speed the Plough, so called after the custom of decorating ploughs and taking them to church to be blessed each spring. However, after such a Godless murder, it was decided to drop the word 'God'. In fact, the pub is usually known as either 'The Plough' (by Worcester folk), or 'The Speed' (by Droitwich folk).

Next to the site of the old 'Snug' is a tiny dining room, used mainly by the licensee's family. A short flight of steps leads down into the kitchen, a modern extension.

Margaret and her husband have been the licensees since 1981. About two years after she arrived, Margaret had an uncanny experience.

It was summer time in the days when the pubs had to close at 10 pm. I work in the kitchen by myself, I had finished serving and was washing up at the kitchen sink when I felt that somebody was there. I turned round and saw this person at the top of the stairs.

It was a male, he was the back end of thirty or early forties and he was tallish, although he may have looked taller than he actually was because he was looking down at me from the top of the stairs. He was slim and his shoes were patent leather (very shiny) with large square buckles on. He had knee socks, black trousers, a tail coat, a rough shirt and a three-cornered hat. His face was thin with deep set eyes, a straight nose and a square jaw.

I felt that he was looking for someone, the expression that he had when he looked at me seemed to say, 'I'm looking for someone but it's not you!' I was not at all frightened, I never wanted to scream or felt nervous. I felt that he was a nice, friendly person.

I only saw him for a few seconds but he was as clear as you are now. Although this happened so many years ago, I sometimes still feel that he is around.

Some months later an artist called at the pub and was able to draw a likeness of the ghost from Margaret's description. The question is: was it Captain Evans? The tricorn hat and large square buckles on shoes faded out after about 1780. Captain Evans was seventy at the time of the murder —did she see him as a younger man or was it someone else that she saw?

☎ **01684 592551**

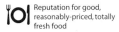 Mediterranean-style
Brasserie (a la carte):
Mon–Sun: 1200–1400
1900–2100
Licensed coffee shop:
0930–1700

 Reputation for good,
reasonably-priced, totally
fresh food

🍺 A local ale is available
known as 'Hook Norton'.

 Accommodation: Ten en
suite rooms. Awards:
Three stars and one
rosette (AA).

White Lion Hotel

LOOKING AT THE SERENE ELEGANCE OF THIS CLASSICAL GEORGIAN FRONT, NO-ONE WOULD GUESS THAT IT HAS TAKEN PART IN SOME OF THE MOST EXCITING MOMENTS IN ENGLISH HISTORY, NOR THAT ONE OF WORCESTERSHIRE'S GREAT VILLAINS PROBABLY MURDERED ONE OF HIS VICTIMS HERE IN THE SEVENTEENTH CENTURY. THE GEORGIAN FRONT ITSELF IS ONLY A FACADE AND MUCH OF THE BUILDING BEHIND IS THOUGHT TO GO BACK TO THE EARLY 1500'S. IT HAS A WEALTH OF MEDIEVAL TIMBERS, ESPECIALLY IN THE WILD GOOSE AND THE ROSE ROOMS. THIS IS WHERE HENRY FIELDING SET THE CLIMACTIC EVENTS OF TOM JONES, TOM SLEPT IN THE WILD GOOSE WHILE THE LOVE OF HIS LIFE, SOPHIA, OCCUPIED THE ROSE.

The whole building is of interest, the car park was once part of a cattle market and the stalls are still marked out on the cobbles. One of the cellars has an unexplored passageway and another has three steps leading to a blocked doorway.

The famous actress, Sarah Siddons (1755-1831), performed in a barn at the back of the inn and this theatrical tradition was continued when the cast of the BBC's 'Tom Jones' stayed here in May 1997 which included Max Beesley, Samantha Morton, Brian Blessed and Francis Delatour.

At the beginning of the civil war, Prince Rupert visited Upton-on-Severn and 'ordered refreshment for his troops at the tavern known as the White Lion'. Towards the end of the war, in 1651, its first class food and ale were responsible for a serious loss to the Royalists. The bridge across the River Severn had been destroyed and replaced by a single plank bridge. A small contingent of soldiers had been designated to guard the bridge but they could not resist the 'propinquity of the Lion Tavern ... Thus heavy sleep came upon the sentinels' so that a group of Parliamentarians were able to cross the bridge and capture the Church. They held out until reinforcements arrived, fierce fighting ensued and the Royalists were forced to retreat to Worcester. A week later, the Royalists were defeated at Worcester in the last great battle of the war.

Ladies will be disappointed to hear that the ghost is not thought to be that of Tom Jones, but of the infamous Captain Bounds. He was a churchwarden in 1640 and fought for the God-fearing Parliamentarians, but later turned to a life of crime. A female body found in one of the top storey rooms was thought to be one of his victims. E M Lawson wrote in 1869:

He was a terrible wicked and cruel man, who married three wives and murdered two, and forged the will of an old lady to get her farm at 'Southend'. The old lady's ghost then began to haunt him and he drowned himself in a pool by the causeway. His ghost then began to haunt the area and was very troublesome. The minister laid him under a great stone that formed part of the little bridge by the pool but he was soon loose again.

The present owner and his wife, Jon and Chris arrived in May 1997. Chris says:

This is a very creaky place upstairs and I don't like going down into the cellar. The previous manager told us that the ghost of Captain Bounds was well-known here. One morning, a resident came down and said, 'Do you have a ghost?' Wondering if he had came face to face with the terrible Captain Bounds, we nervously admitted that there were rumours. It turned out that he had seen the ghost of a cat in his room.

There is a story that one of the guests woke up in the night and felt that someone was shaking hands with him. This, surely, would have been Tom Jones and not the infamous Captain Bounds.

the Boat

IN ALL MY YEARS I HAVE WORKED AT A BREWERY I HAVE NEVER BEFORE OR SINCE HAD THE KIND OF EXPERIENCE I HAD AT THE BOAT.

It was a newish pub having been recently rebuilt, and I moved there in about 1982. Whilst I was landlord, I won a prize for the best English pint and platter.

Our Company Director, Terry Thomson, who unfortunately is no longer with us, said to me, 'Do you know the story about the Boat?'. Then he told me that during the war, when they had guns at Oakham in Tividale, the Germans were going over and these guns were firing shells. One shell went up and came down again, right down the chimney of the Boat and straight into the cellar. A young girl who had just got married and other people were in the pub. It killed the bride and blew the groom's arm off. This bloke was telling me that that was how he got his wooden leg. He was only about 5 or 6 but he was at the reception and he had his leg blown off.

Some years later, I had forgotten all about this story when I was working in the pub late one Friday night. The pub had closed down and my only company was Jason, my German Shepherd. I thought to myself, 'Right, I have got to clear the lines out ready for the weekend' so first I was working in the cellar getting everything prepared, then I was cleaning the pipes out behind the bar. From where I was working I could see into the lounge where the lights were off and I was one hundred percent sober!

SUDDENLY, THE DOG MADE A NOISE, HIS HAIR STOOD STRAIGHT UP ON END AND HE RAN OFF. I HAVE NEVER KNOWN HIM DO THAT BEFORE OR SINCE. I HAD A COLD FEELING, RIGHT DOWN MY BACK, AS IF THE HAIR ON MY BACK WAS STANDING UP. THEN MY COLLECTION OF BOTTLE TOPS HANGING BEHIND THE BAR STARTED TO RATTLE AND WERE SWINGING BACKWARDS AND FORWARDS. I THOUGHT, 'MY GOD, WHAT'S HAPPENING?'.

I LOOKED UP INTO THE LOUNGE AND I SAW A WHITE MIST. IT CAME FROM ONE END OF THE LOUNGE TOWARDS ME, WENT ACROSS IN FRONT OF THE BAR AND AS IT GOT TO THE OTHER END OF THIS ROOM IT TOTALLY DISAPPEARED. IT WAS LIKE A WEDDING VEIL, SO FAINT THAT YOU COULD SEE THROUGH IT. YOU COULDN'T HEAR ANYTHING, IT FLOATED OVER AND THEN IT HAD GONE. I THOUGHT, 'AM I DREAMING?' AND I HASTILY SWITCHED EVERYTHING OFF BEFORE I RUSHED OFF TO BED.

I NEVER STAYED DOWN THERE LATE AT NIGHT AGAIN. IT WAS SOMETHING THAT I SHALL NEVER EVER FORGET AS LONG AS I LIVE.

☎ 0121 557 5653

Mon–Sun:
Bar: Open all day
Food: Reasonable times

Large patio area

Special beers are Banks's, Fosters and a few lagers

A special event is organised about once a month such as a Karaoke evening or a bonfire night in November.

his hair stood on end and he shot out of the kitchen

WEBHEATH

Foxlydiate Hotel

THE FOXLYDIATE USED TO BE FOXLYDIATE HOUSE AND THE OLD FOX AND GOOSE PUB WAS NEARBY. THE FOX AND GOOSE WAS DEMOLISHED AND THE LICENCE TAKEN TO THE FOXLYDIATE HOTEL. HEWELL GRANGE IS ABOUT HALF-A-MILE AWAY, ONCE A RESIDENCE OF THE EARL OF PLYMOUTH IT IS NOW OCCUPIED BY HM OFFENDERS.

One of the elderly ladies who has lived in the area all her life says that her mother told her the following story:

Sometime near the turn of the last century, a maid from Hewell Grange nearby was having an affair with someone at the Fox and Goose. The illicit relationship was discovered by the maid's husband who stabbed her to death. The deed was done, so they say. If you look carefully you can still see the remains of the lovers' track which runs from Hewell Grange to where the Fox and Goose once stood, close by the Foxlydiate, and if you happen to pass that way on dark nights you may be able to see the wife, the white lady of the Foxlydiate, who wanders up and down the path and into the pub. The ghost was seen so often and was so well known, that when I first started work at fourteen and had to cycle up those country lanes, I was terrified.

One of the old regulars says:

Three previous landlords thought that the Foxlydiate was haunted. In about 1940 the Fox and Goose was a Dares Pub and the manager was a Harry Powell. He 'swore blind' the place was haunted. His wife said that she was once pushed down the stairs. Mr Davey took over the tenancy for five or six years and his barman was a Scotch man named Alex who had a dog, Sonner. Alex used to be in the kitchen all evening, then he would go upstairs for a meal. Alex said that one night, he was sitting there, and he was just going to have his meal when Sonner started howling, his hair stood on end and he shot out of the kitchen.

Mr Palmer was another licensee who used to tell everybody that the place was haunted.

One story reached the ears of the local paper in the summer of 1990. When a painter and decorator was stripping the walls, a silhouette of a woman showed through. He papered over the silhouette but it still showed through.

01527 542934

Situated just off the Bromsgrove to Redditch highway. Take the exit for Blakenhurst prison and follow the signs to Webheath

Non-residents:
Mon–Sun:
Bar: 1130–2300
Food: 1200–2130

Two separate children's areas

An extensive menu complemented by home-cooked specials, bar snacks are also available

Large garden

Owned by the Greenalls' Group, it has 33 en-suite rooms

WEBHEATH

a young woman was trapped in the room and burned to death

WORCESTER

Cardinal's Hat

WORCESTER MAY SEEM A BUSY CITY TODAY, but this is nothing to the hordes of visitors arriving in medieval times. There were, for example, the thousands of pilgrims hoping for a miracle at the tombs of Saint Oswald and Saint Wulstan. There were also the traders bringing and taking goods along the River Severn and the River Teme, as the few roads in existence were usually nothing more than dirt tracks. Many of these people needed some kind of hospitality, consequently some of today's hotels and public houses date back to medieval times.

Those with ecclesiastical signs, such as the Cardinals' Hat, are most likely to be the oldest. Records of the Cardinal's Hat start at 1518, but a house was built on the site long before then. In the mid 1700's the name had to be changed to the Swan and Falcon because Roman Catholics (and therefore Cardinals) became very unpopular after a rebellion of 1745. In 1804 it became the Coventry Arms to flatter the Earl of Coventry, but in the 1950's the original name was restored.

In the winter of 1991, Rob Talbot Cooper arrived to take over as manager. About three weeks after he had moved in, he decided to unpack some boxes which he had stored in a small room at the top of the house. It was obviously the old servant's quarters, with the tiniest of fire grates set in a miniature chimney breast.

At first it was quite chilly, but after I had been working a short time, I realised I was sweating a lot. The increase in temperature hadn't been noticeable but by the time I left the room it was steaming hot. The corridor outside was quite cold, and when I returned a minute or two later the room was cold again. I thought nothing of it at the time, but just thought that I was having a hot flush or something.

Some weeks later I heard the story that, at the turn of the century, a young woman was trapped in the room and burned to death. Her ghost is said to manifest itself by a sudden rise in temperature. I have had the same experience four or five times, and friends who have stayed in the house, but did not know the story, have felt it. Previous tenants tell me that they also have felt this strange heat.

☎ **01905 22222**

➜ Friar Streeet

🕐 Mon–Sat: 1100–2300
Sun: 1230–2230

👤 Yes

🍴 Home-cooked

⛱ Patio area

🍺 Four guest ales

ⓘ Owned by the Wolverhampton and Dudley Breweries

Ye Olde Talbot Hotel

☎ 01905 23573

➡ Across the road from the Cathedral

Non-residents:
Mon–Sun: normal

Value-for-money dishes and Sunday lunch

ⓘ The hotel has a conference room and 29 en suite bedrooms all with Sky TV. An attractive bar and oak-panelled restaurant crammed with antiques.

THE FOREFRONT OF THE CATHEDRAL WAS ONCE MUCH LARGER THAN IT IS NOW, AND INCLUDED THE BUILDING NOW KNOWN AS YE OLDE TALBOT HOTEL, PARTS OF WHICH COULD BE AS MUCH AS 800 YEARS OLD. DURING THE FIFTEENTH CENTURY IT WAS AN ECCLESIASTICAL INN KNOWN AS A CHURCH HOUSE. IT WAS RE-OPENED AFTER REFURBISHMENT IN 1980.

The housekeeper, Jan, does not believe in ghosts and has to be persuaded to tell her story.

I think that people only see ghosts if they want to see them, and I must say that I have not seen anything before or since this incident. However, there was absolutely no mistaking what I saw that day.

It happened in about 1990, I remember that I had not been working here for very long. Going into room 14 (which is one of the smaller ones) I turned back to prop the door open, then, continuing into the room, I saw on an armless chair by the window, a big black cat. It was sleek and healthy with shiny fur and big green eyes, obviously well looked after. It had raised its head and was looking towards the door, as a cat would when someone enters a room and wakes it. I called to the girls, 'There's a cat in this room', but when I looked back it had gone. The window was not open and it definitely did not pass me. We hunted high and low but there was no cat. When I went downstairs I said:

I'VE JUST SEEN
THE ghost of a cat

and then several people told me that the hotel is supposed to be haunted by a cat. It usually appears between 10 and 10.30 am, most often on the stairs or in the bar. One of the bartenders, William Miller, said that it looked like a large bundle of steel wool which faded after a second or two. It terrified his dog.

This apparition of a cat has been seen by the previous manager, his wife and various guests.

WORCESTER

WORCESTER

Café Rouge

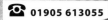

...THE PANS MANAGED TO GET FROM ONE END OF THE VERY LONG BAR TO THE OTHER WITHOUT SETTING OFF THE ALARM

DESPITE THE FRENCH NAME, this is an old Worcester restaurant and is known to have existed as long ago as 1408. It stood at the north-western edge of Greyfriars Monastery and has been used chiefly as a bakery and baker's shop. Over the centuries parts have been extended and adjacent buildings assimilated, so that it is now a charming hotchpotch of oak beams, unexpected steps and uneven floors. To the rear is a tiny yard, enclosed by buildings but open to the sky, and leading off this is the small dry store and a larger cellar which has recently been refrigerated.

For two years, Cafe Rouge (when it was known as Bottles Wine Bar) was plagued by a poltergeist. It began just before Christmas 1994, when the cellar out the back was fitted with huge refrigerators, previously it had been the store room for wine and bottled beers.

In the autumn of 1994 a new member of staff started work at Bottles Wine Bar and, on the Thursday afternoon, she was left on her own to mind the bar. To the right of the bar and almost behind it is a flight of wooden steps, leading to a balcony above. She was tidying up one or two odds and ends, half-listening to the background music, when suddenly she was surprised to hear slow, heavy footsteps ascending the wooden steps and walking along the balcony. She came out of bar and turned round to look up at the staircase to see who was

there, and to her horror, found it quite empty. Fortunately, her boyfriend worked in a shop a few doors down the road, so she telephoned him and insisted that he stayed with her for the remainder of the afternoon. She then left and refused to come back.

Nicky, the manager, said that all the staff heard the footsteps but they didn't bother about them.

Until recently the poltergeist has not been much of a problem. We did have strange things happening but they were very few and far between. My first experience of it came at the end of one night when I had only been here a few days. As a rookie (newest member of staff), instead of sitting with the others and having a drink after we had closed, I had to sweep and clean the bar floor. I finished mopping and went outside, for only a few seconds, to take the mop. When I came back all the buckets, which had been behind the bar, were dragged into the middle of the bar. I thought someone was playing a joke on me but everyone laughed at the idea that they would do such a stupid thing. In any case the floor was wet and if anyone had walked on it I would have seen their footsteps. No-one had heard anything either and buckets are quite noisy items to move. I didn't think much about it, I was more annoyed than anything.

A day or two later I went into the

cellar and was literally in there for just two seconds. When I came out there was a crate of bottles right in the doorway, in fact I tripped over them. Almost the next day I saw, with my own eyes, a keg in the dry store fall over, roll across the floor then stand up again. It was unbelievable. It hadn't hit anything. Then, about a week after the refrigerators had been installed, they failed to work and we had to get the engineer out. He said that he couldn't understand it, someone had turned the refrigerator off but it couldn't have been any of the staff because it's quite a complicated operation and you needed a special spanner to do it which, of course, we didn't have.

We keep a set of frying pans in the kitchen, all stacked one on top of the other, and one morning about this time, I arrived at work to find that the pans were stacked behind the front door. I had to push them with the door in order to get in. The strange thing is that we have an alarm which is activated by any movement and the pans managed to get from one end of the very long bar to the other without setting off the alarm. We were very busy, it was just before Christmas, and we found these incidents very frustrating.

One Friday night, one of the staff had left his bike out in the yard. There's always a strange wind in that yard, it must be some kind of wind tunnel. At about 10.30 that evening I went out the back, noticed the bike outside and thought it would have been better under cover in the cellar, but I decided not to move it. An hour later this person went out to get his bike to find that it had been moved into the cellar. None of us had been out and there is no public access to that area - it's surrounded by high walls.

Gemma, the Duty Manager, adds:

Nicky's last incident shows the way in which whatever-it-is reads our minds. It often does that. I was closing up one night and I said to Nicky, 'I'm going to turn the CD off now!' As I said it, the CD turned itself off! It was off for about ten seconds then it turned itself on again. On another occasion we were thinking of playing a practical joke on one of the staff. Although he's over six feet tall he's quite nervous of our ghost, so we thought that we would arrange some of the furniture half way down the stairs, as if the ghost had thrown it down. In the end, we decided not to do this—we thought it would be too scary. Two days later when we turned up for work this is exactly what had happened—the furniture was halfway down the stairs.

Sometimes, an incident is quite amusing - there was the time I was sitting on the loo when I heard someone tapping on the wall, it sounded as if they were tapping on tiles with a key. Occasionally, it can be quite frightening. I was going up the steps to the balcony one night when I heard a howl right behind me. I thought a cat had got in but when I turned round, nothing was there. Sometimes, when I go into the yard I hear a young woman give a terrible scream. It only lasts for a second or two but it's quite chilling.

Opposite the bar is a line of six small dining tables and every table has a lighted candle in the centre. I was standing behind the bar last week when I saw each candle go out, one by one, as if someone was walking past the tables, snuffing each one out as he went past.

However, most of the time the poltergeist is simply a nuisance. It messes about with the electrics, the lights flash and we have that many light bulbs going all the time. Just a few minutes ago I went into the dry store and before I could switch the light on, it had flashed on and gone off again. There's a large walk-in cupboard off the storeroom where the heating controls are. One night, we couldn't get the heating to work. Just as we walked back through it went on and off again.

I was sceptical about these things until I came here. I've now changed my mind!

☎ 01905 26204

→ Sidbury, near Commandery

Mon–Sat: 1200–2300
Sun: 1200–2230

Allowed in the back

Banks's beers.

ⓘ Has bands every weekend, Rock and Blues, with Showcases on a Sunday.

Kings Head

THE KINGS HEAD IS BUILT ON THE SITE OF CITY GATE, AT SIDBURY, WHERE ONCE A GREAT DITCH HAD BEEN DUG AS PART OF THE FORTIFICATIONS FOR THE BATTLE OF WORCESTER IN 1651. THE SCENE HERE WAS SO TERRIBLE AFTER THE BATTLE, WITH BODIES STACKED UP AGAINST THE SIDBURY GATE, THAT THE AREA WAS LEFT DEVASTATED FOR AT LEAST FIFTY YEARS. THE FUTURE CHARLES II WAS VERY LUCKY TO ESCAPE WITH HIS LIFE. HE WAS ON FOOT BRAVELY TRYING TO RALLY HIS MEN OUTSIDE THE COMMANDERY WHEN A MOUNTED PARLIAMEN-TARIAN RECOGNISED HIM AND RUSHED AT HIM. WILLIAM BAGNALL, A WORCESTER CITIZEN, QUICKLY SEIZED THE BRIDLE OF A TEAM OF OXEN PULLING AN AMMUNITION WAGGON AND DRAGGED THEM ACROSS THE ROAD, PREVENTING THE PARLIAMENTARIAN FROM DOING HIS WORST AND ENABLING CHARLES TO SLIP THROUGH A NARROW GAP AND ESCAPE. IT IS NO WONDER THAT THREE INNS IN SIDBURY, YE OLDE TALBOT, THE BARLEY MOW AND THE KINGS HEAD HAVE GHOST STORIES TO TELL.

Ralph Cooper had been the licensee of the Kings Head for fourteen months in the August of 1982, when he reported to the *Worcester Evening News* that the pub was frequently visited by an apparition commonly known as 'Sid'. He usually manifested himself by turning off barrels of beer, ringing the 'Time' bell and tilting pictures. However, he had been known to walk through walls wearing a leather jerkin and pantaloons, to appear to startled customers. His last appearance had been six weeks previously when he appeared to a Swedish tourist and warned him in French of future danger. Next day the Swede was beaten up.

The present licensee, Barry, arrived in April 1997 and has so far not come across anything strange but says he is keeping his eyes open.

WORCESTER

WORCESTER, SIDBURY

Barley Mow

☎ 01905 351166

→ Sidbury. Near Commandery but further from town centre

⊘ Mon–Sat: 1200–2300
Sun: 1200–2230

⦿ Bar snacks

🍺 Four real ales

ⓘ A disco every Sunday from 1500–1900

THE BARLEY MOW HAS A VICTORIAN FRONTAGE BUT THE BACK IS MUCH OLDER.

The licensees from 1971 until 1992 were George and Angela Barrett. They had four daughters and Michelle, the eldest, says:

When my parents first moved there, we had a club room on the first floor, but later we had it converted into a living room. This is where our ghost lived. He was a friendly entity and I think he was attracted to people because he liked to make his presence known. He was continually opening the club room door and we could hear his footsteps in there, they were definitely a man's footsteps and they sounded as if they were walking on lino. We grew quite fond of our ghost and we called him Fred. Although Fred was mainly in the club room, he did visit other parts of the house. In the bedrooms, you would feel that someone was watching you. Things would disappear from all over the house, particularly belts and shoes - with four girls this was only to be expected, but items like glasses would also disappear which you knew you had left in a certain place in the bar. Sometimes he would move one of your possessions; there would be, say, a comb on the dressing table, you would blink and it would be somewhere else.

Mrs Barrett, a sensible, down-to-earth woman, gives further details:

There's no doubt that the place was haunted. As you worked in the kitchen downstairs you would feel that someone was walking behind you. Bottles would rattle violently for no reason. We would often find that the gas in the cellar had been turned off. Outside was a built-in yard and somebody came in once and said that there was a whirlwind in the yard and everything was flying round.

Once I was in the cellar and the door slammed shut and I couldn't open it. Fortunately, there is another way out so I was able to go round and come out the other way. That has never happened before or since. It was very eerie.

My husband was showing somebody out late one night and there were only two people there, my husband and this other person. Suddenly, the visitor said, 'There's somebody behind you'. He said that the ghost appeared to be going down steps behind the bar but there are no steps. He said that the ghost looked like a long-haired yobbo, but we have assumed that it was a Cavalier because of Worcester's association with the Royalists.

Welcome Inn

Up for sale in July 1988

IN THE HEART OF WORCESTER A TINY ROAD, WYLDE LANE, LEADS OFF SIDBURY TO A PUBLIC HOUSE WHICH SINCE 1996 HAS BEEN KNOWN AS THE WELCOME INN.

Before then it was known as the Lamplighter and previously it was the Garibaldi, so-named by Richard Padmore, MP, who laid out the local Coles Hill estate in 1860 and to whom Garibaldi was a hero.

Perhaps the previous owners of the Garibaldi hoped that a change of name would shake off the memories of its terrible past, for in this building almost an entire family were murdered.

Ernest Laight was appointed as licensee of the Garibaldi in 1925 and he soon became very friendly with a local policeman, Herbert Burrows, who came from London and had just completed his seven month probationary period. On Friday, 27 November 1925, Burrows arrived at the local station and said, 'What about those terrible murders at the Garibaldi?'. No-one at the station knew anything about them but it was not long before they were called to the inn. A dreadful scene met their eyes:

The bloody bodies of the landlady and her husband were in the cellar, while upstairs a baby had been battered to death. A second child, a six-year old, had not been touched and had slept peacefully through it all. By that first remark, Burrows was implicated in the murder; he eventually confessed and was executed in 1926. The locals say that Burrows had been having an affair with the landlady.

The internal construction of the Welcome Inn has now been changed so that it is one large room. At one end is an archway at right angles to an outside wall where there was once a hatch to the street and local people brought their jugs to be filled with beer. Before the arch was inserted this was the wall of a passageway which led upstairs to where some of the murders were committed.

The locals say that the ghost of a woman and a child has been seen there. Andy, the present barman, says:

I find this a very spooky place. All cellars are cold, but this one is exceptionally cold. As well, when I'm downstairs I can hear bumps and thuds upstairs and I know that no-one is up there.

almost *an entire family* were **MURDERED**

WORCESTER

WHEN THEY WERE IN THE CELLAR, strange things happened

☎ **01905 22344**

➡ St Nicholas Street at
N. end of City Walls Road

🕐 Mon–Sat: 1200–2300
Sun: 1200 for a
few hours

🧍 Yes

🍴🅾🍴 Varied menu including
balti

🍺 Guest ale

ⓘ There are three letting
rooms and the piped
background music is
usually light jazz. The
bartender tells us that
this pub was very popular
with Americans during
the second world war.

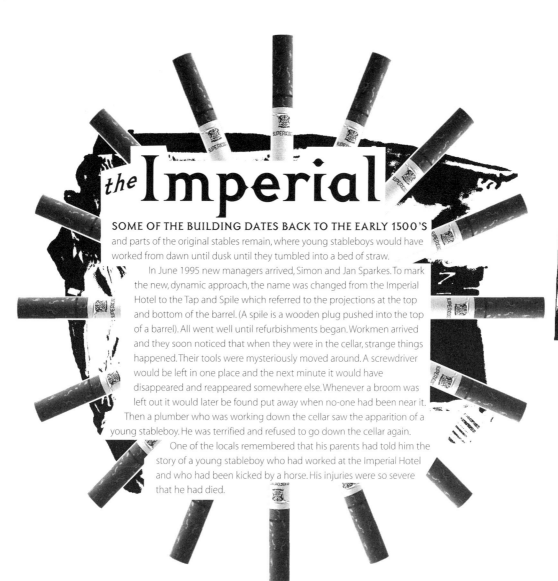

the Imperial

SOME OF THE BUILDING DATES BACK TO THE EARLY 1500'S

and parts of the original stables remain, where young stableboys would have worked from dawn until dusk until they tumbled into a bed of straw.

In June 1995 new managers arrived, Simon and Jan Sparkes. To mark the new, dynamic approach, the name was changed from the Imperial Hotel to the Tap and Spile which referred to the projections at the top and bottom of the barrel. (A spile is a wooden plug pushed into the top of a barrel). All went well until refurbishments began. Workmen arrived and they soon noticed that when they were in the cellar, strange things happened. Their tools were mysteriously moved around. A screwdriver would be left in one place and the next minute it would have disappeared and reappeared somewhere else. Whenever a broom was left out it would later be found put away when no-one had been near it. Then a plumber who was working down the cellar saw the apparition of a young stableboy. He was terrified and refused to go down the cellar again.

One of the locals remembered that his parents had told him the story of a young stableboy who had worked at the Imperial Hotel and who had been kicked by a horse. His injuries were so severe that he had died.

Vine Inn

THE VINE INN IS ONE OF THE OLDEST PUBS IN NORTHWICK. IT WAS LISTED IN 1873 AS AN INN AND REOPENED AFTER RENOVATIONS IN 1980. ITS SITUATION ON THE OMBERSLEY ROAD IS EXPLAINED BY THE FACT THAT THE TRAM TERMINUS WAS ONCE OUTSIDE.

The ample car park and roomy lounge make it an ideal place for meetings. Two darts teams meet here, one of them national, as well as cricket teams, quiz teams, crib teams, a deep sea angling club and the local labour party.

The Vine Inn has the reputation of being haunted which is explained by Syd, a regular of 47 years standing.

Just after the second world war the landlady here was a Maggie Scott, a buxom piece, although her husband was a very small fellow. She employed a young barman who went missing one Sunday afternoon and it was discovered that he had collapsed in the cellar. He was carried upstairs where he died. After that Maggie always swore that she could see his ghost in the cellar.

The present licensee, Bob, and his wife celebrated eleven years at the Vine on 9 September 1997. Bob comes from Glasgow but his wife was born in the next street. He says that on three occasions things have happened which he could not explain, all of which were in the cellar. He says:

We sell traditional beer all pumped up by hand with the exception of the lager beers and the Guinness. I came down one morning and opened up at 11 o'clock. At 11.30 all my pumps ceased to function. There is a certain sequence of events that you go through when this happens and your first action is to look at the gas. The gas cylinders were all turned off. No way could this happen by accident and no-one could have gone down there. I never get so drunk that I would turn them off myself without knowing.

This happened twice in the first year that I was here, then the latest was sometime in April of 1997.

☎ **01905 456158**

➜ On the A449 Ombersley Road, not far from the large island near Claines

🕐 Mon–Sat: 1100–1430
1730–2300
Sun: 1100–1430
1730–2230

🍺 Davenport's traditional, landlord describes it as 'the best beer in town'

ⓘ Owned by Greenall's. Won the 'Worcester in Bloom' competition for five consecutive years and came second on the other years. It received a commendation from the brewery.

THE VINE

Ketch Inn

☎ 01905 820269

➜ The Ketch stands on a cliff overlooking the River Severn and can be seen from the new Malvern/Worcester by-pass

🕐 Mon–Sat: 1100–2300
Sun: 1200–2250

🚹 Children welcome, there is an indoor (Wacky Warehouse) and outdoor children's play area

🍴 Bar and restaurant

⚘ Patio with chairs and tables

☕ Tetley and Pedigree beers

ⓘ Owned by Allied Domeq Leisure

IN THE SEVENTEENTH CENTURY, WHEN EVENTS WERE HOTTING UP WHICH LED TO THE

Battle of Worcester, the Ketch was known as the Pig and Whistle and was a watering hole for Oliver Cromwell's troops. The old pub lies underneath the cellar of the present pub.

The Ketch was featured in the Worcester Evening News on 1st February, 1989. Since the landlord, Maurice Corey, had taken over in 1987, doors mysteriously opened by themselves, lights went on and off and …

CUTLERY at the breakfast table in an EMPTY dining ROOM was found to have been BENT.

His two guard dogs refused to go into the cellar and a Scottish guest left in panic when his belongings threw themselves round his room. Maurice was unconvinced until one morning, he found all the bar windows wide open, when he was certain that he had closed them the previous evening.

He called in a medium, who said that a barmaid had been raped by an ostler who worked at the pub about 140 years ago. When the baby was born he killed the child and murdered the mother.

Her ghost still haunts The Ketch today where she is known as Olive. She opens windows and turns the lights on and off. She is thought to live in the cellar, where most of the problems occur. Time and time again the staff find that the gases or the lines canisters have been mysteriously turned off.

WORCESTER · BROOMHALL

bibliography

Bladys of the Stewponey (The), S Baring-Gould, 1897, Dudley archive collection, Coseley.

Civil War in Worcestershire (The) and **Scotch Invasion of 1651** (The), J W Willis Bund, 1979, Alan Sutton.

Haunted Pub Guide (The), Guy Lyon Playfair, 1985, Javelin Books.

Haunted Pubs in Britain and Ireland, Marc Alexander, 1984, publisher unknown.

Midland Ghosts and Hauntings, Anne Bradford and Barrie Roberts, 1994, John Roberts of Quercus.

Pubs and Breweries of the Old Dudley Borough (The), John Richards, 1989, Real Ale Books.

Pub Walks in Worcestershire, Richard Shurey, 1993, Countryside Books.

Worcestershire Village Book (The), 1992, Countryside Books and Worcestershire Federation of Women's Institutes.

Further sources Deeds, wills and Abstracts of Titles, Hereford and Worcester archives.

John Richards makes a professional search for pub history and I have at times used his framed pub history hanging on a pub wall.

Bill Gwillam has produced two excellent gazetteers on Worcestershire pubs which are in Worcester public library. Several licencees have mentioned that they don't know anything about their history and I suggest that they look in these gazetteers. There is a sentence or two about most old hostelries.